OLD MO

HOROSCOPE AND ASTRAL DIARY

LIBRA

foulsham
LONDON • NEW YORK • TORONTO • SYDNEY

foulsham

Capital Point, 33 Bath Road, Slough, Berkshire, SL1 3UF,
England

Foulsham books can be found in all good bookshops and direct from
www.foulsham.com

ISBN: 978-0-572-04008-6

A CIP record for this book is available from the British Library

Printed in Great Britain by CPI Group (UK) Ltd, Croydon, CR0 4YY.

CONTENTS

INTRODUCTION

In the midst of our busy lives we often fail to notice the subtle changes within our natures that take place on an almost moment-by-moment basis. Some of these are the natural result of circumstances, but others are a direct response to the constantly changing patterns of the Sun, Moon and planets. Astrology gives us an opportunity to make the very best of what cosmological forces are acting upon us at any particular point in time, and Old Moore has been tracking planetary movements and the bearing they have on humanity for many centuries. The most recent result of his efforts is the Astral Diary for 2013 – a complete book geared specifically towards you and the influences that help to make you what you are.

If you want to know whether a new relationship is likely to turn out the way you hope, whether you are in for a good time in the financial stakes, or whether family pressures could be a problem, Old Moore is the person to ask. The Astral Diary gives you an easy-to-follow daily summary of the way the stars and planets are affecting you, and also tells you what you should be doing now in order to maximise your potential for the future. And there is also space in the diaries for your own comments and appointments.

The Astral Diary allows you to look much deeper into your own individual nature than other yearly forecasts do. Your uniqueness is reflected by the time of day you were born and by the position of specific heavenly bodies such as the Moon and the planet Venus. Using the Astral Diary's unique tables you can work out what makes you tick in a much more personal sense, and can then deal much more effectively with the twists and turns of life.

Every nuance of your nature is captured within your astrological profile, and using the Astral Diary you can get so close to the core of planetary influence that you can almost feel the subtle undertones that, in the end, have a profound bearing on your life and circumstances. It is even possible to register when little Mercury is 'retrograde', which means that it appears to be moving backwards in space when viewed from the Earth. Mercury rules communication, so be prepared to deal with a few setbacks in this area when you see the sign ☿. Used correctly, astrology allows you to maximise your potential, to strike whilst the iron is hot and to live a more contented and successful life. Consulting *Old Moore's Astral Diary* will make you more aware of what really makes you the person you are and is a fascinating way to register the very heartbeat of the solar system of which we are all a part.

Old Moore extends his customary greeting to all people of the Earth and offers his age-old wishes for a happy and prosperous period ahead.

THE ESSENCE OF LIBRA

Exploring the Personality of Libra the Scales

(24th SEPTEMBER – 23rd OCTOBER)

What's in a sign?

At heart you may be the least complicated of all the zodiac sign types, though your ruling element is Air, and that is always going to supply some surprises. Diplomatic, kind and affectionate, your nature blows like a refreshing breeze through the lives of almost anyone you meet. It isn't like you to be gloomy for very long at a time, and you know how to influence the world around you.

It's true that you don't like dirt, or too much disorganisation, and you tend to be very artistic by inclination. You get your own way in life, not by dint of making yourself unpopular in any way but rather with the sort of gentle persuasion to which almost everyone you know falls victim at one time or another. Being considerate of others is more or less second nature to you, though you may not be quite as self-sacrificing as sometimes appears to be the case. You definitely know what you want from life and are not above using a little subterfuge when it comes to getting it.

You are capable and resourceful, but just a little timid on occasions. All the same, when dealing with subject matter that you know and relish, few can better you out there in the practical world. You know how to order your life and can be just as successful in a career sense as you tend to be in your home life. There are times when personal attractions can be something of a stumbling block because you love readily and are very influenced by the kindness and compliments of those around you.

Librans do need to plan ahead, but don't worry about this fact too much because you are also extremely good at thinking on your feet. Getting others to do your bidding is a piece of cake because you are not tardy when it comes to showing your affections. Nevertheless you need to be careful not to allow yourself to fall into unreliable company, or to get involved in schemes that seem too good to be true – some of them are. But for most of the time you present a happy picture to the world and get along just fine, with your ready smile and adaptable personality. You leave almost any situation happier and more contented than it was when you arrived.

Libra resources

When it comes to getting on in life you have as much ammunition in your armoury as most zodiac signs and a great deal more than some. For starters you are adaptable and very resourceful. When you have to take a leap in logic there is nothing preventing you from doing so, and the strong intuition of which your zodiac sign is capable can prove to be very useful at times.

One of your strongest points is the way you manage to make others love you. Although you might consider yourself to be distinctly 'ordinary', that's not the way the world at large perceives you. Most Librans have the ability to etch themselves onto the minds of practically everyone they come across. Why? It's simple. You listen to what people have to say and appear to be deeply interested. On most occasions you are, but even if the tale is a tedious one you give the impression of being rooted to the spot with a determination to hear the story right through. When it comes to responding you are extremely diplomatic and always manage to steer a sensible course between any two or more opposing factions.

Having said that you don't like dirt or untidy places, this is another fact that you can turn to your advantage, because you can always find someone who will help you out. So charming can Libra be that those who do all they can to make you more comfortable regularly end up feeling that you have done them a favour.

It is the sheer magic of the understated Libran that does the trick every time. Even on those rare occasions when you go out with all guns blazing to get what you want from life, you are very unlikely to make enemies on the way. Of course you do have to be careful on occasions, like everyone, but you can certainly push issues further than most. Why? Mainly because people don't realise that you are doing so.

You could easily sell any commodity – though it might be necessary to believe in it yourself first. Since you can always see the good points in anything and tend to be generally optimistic, that should not be too problematical either.

Beneath the surface

In many respects Libra could be the least complicated sign of the zodiac so it might be assumed that 'what you see is what you get'. Life is rarely quite that simple, though you are one of the most straightforward people when it comes to inner struggle. The fact is that most Librans simply don't have a great deal. Between subconscious motivation and in-your-face action there is a seamless process. Librans do need to be loved and this fact can be quite a strong motivation in itself towards any particular course of action. However, even this desire for affection isn't the most powerful factor when considering the sign of the Scales.

What matters most to you is balance, which is probably not at all surprising considering what your zodiac sign actually means. Because of this you would go to tremendous lengths to make sure that your inner resolves create the right external signs and actions to offer the peace that you are looking for most of all.

Like most people born under the Air signs you are not quite as confident as you sometimes appear to be. In the main you are modest and not given to boasting, so you don't attract quite the level of attention of your fellow Air signs, Gemini and Aquarius. All the same you are quite capable of putting on an act when it's necessary to give a good account of yourself in public. You could be quaking inside but you do have the ability to hide this from the world at large.

Librans exhibit such a strong desire to be kind to everyone they meet that they may hide their inner feelings from some people altogether. It's important to remember to be basically honest, even if that means upsetting others a little. This is the most difficult trait for Libra to deal with and may go part of the way to explaining why so many relationship break-ups occur for people born under this zodiac sign. However, as long as you find ways and means to explain your deepest emotional needs, at least to those you love, all should be well.

In most respects you tend to be an open book, particularly to those who take the trouble to look. Your nature is not over-deep, and you are almost certainly not on some secret search to find the 'real you'. Although Libra is sometimes accused of being superficial there are many people in the world who would prefer simplicity to complications and duplicity.

Making the best of yourself

This may be the easiest category by far for the zodiac sign of Libra. The fact is that you rarely do anything else but offer the best version of what you are. Presentation is second nature to Libra, which just loves to be noticed. Despite this you are naturally modest and so not inclined to go over the top in company. You can be relied upon to say and do the right things for most of the time. Even when you consider your actions to be zany and perhaps less acceptable, this is not going to be the impression that the majority of people would get.

In a work sense you need to be involved in some sort of occupation that is clean, allows for a sense of order and ultimately offers the ability to use your head as well as your hands. The fact is that you don't care too much for unsavoury sorts of work and need to be in an environment that suits your basically refined nature. If the circumstances are right you can give a great deal to your work and will go far. Librans also need to be involved with others because they are natural co-operators. For this reason you may not be at your best when working alone or in situations that necessitate all the responsibilities being exclusively yours.

When in the social mainstream you tend to make the best of yourself by simply being what you naturally are. You don't need frills and fancies. Libra is able to make the best sort of impression by using the natural qualities inherent in the sign. As a result, your natural poise, your ability to cut through social divisions, your intelligence and your adaptability should all ensure that you remain popular.

What may occasionally prove difficult is being quite as dominant as the world assumes you ought to be. Many people equate efficiency with power. This is not the way of people born under the Scales, and you need to make that fact plain to anyone who seems to have the desire to shape you.

The impressions you give

Although the adage 'what you see is what you get' may be truer for Libra than for any of its companion signs, it can't be exclusively the case. However, under almost all circumstances you are likely to make friends. You are a much shrewder operator than sometimes appears to be the case and tend to weigh things in the balance very carefully. Libra can be most things to most people, and that's the sort of adaptability that ensures success at both a social and a professional level.

The chances are that you are already well respected and deeply liked by most of the people you know. This isn't so surprising since you are not inclined to make waves of any sort. Whether or not this leads to you achieving the degree of overall success that you deserve in life is quite a different matter. When impressions count you don't tend to let yourself down, or the people who rely on you. Adapting yourself to suit different circumstances is the meat and drink of your basic nature and you have plenty of poise and charm to disarm even the most awkward of people.

In affairs of the heart you are equally adept at putting others at their ease. There is very little difficulty involved in getting people to show their affection for you and when it comes to romance you are one of the most successful practitioners to be found anywhere. The only slight problem in this area of life, as with others, is that you are so talented at offering people what they want that you might not always be living the sort of life that genuinely suits you. Maybe giving the right impression is a little too important for Libra. A deeper form of honesty from the start would prevent you from having to show a less charming side to your nature in the end.

In most circumstances you can be relied upon to exhibit a warm, affectionate, kind, sincere and interesting face to the world at large. As long as this underpins truthfulness it's hard to understand how Libra could really go far wrong.

The way forward

You must already be fairly confident that you have the necessary skills and natural abilities to get on well in a world that is also filled with other people. From infancy most Librans learn how to rub along with others, whilst offering every indication that they are both adaptable and amenable to change. Your chameleon-like ability to 'change colour' in order to suit prevailing circumstances means that you occasionally drop back to being part of the wallpaper in the estimation of at least some people. A greater ability to make an impression probably would not go amiss sometimes, but making a big fuss isn't your way and you actively seek an uncomplicated sort of life.

Balance is everything to Libra, a fact that means there are times when you end up with nothing at all. What needs to be remembered is that there are occasions when everyone simply has to make a decision. This is the hardest thing in the world for you to do but when you manage it you become even more noticed by the world at large.

There's no doubt that people generally hold you in great affection. They know you to be quite capable and love your easy-going attitude to life. You are rarely judgmental and tend to offer almost anyone the benefit of the doubt. Although you are chatty, and inclined to listen avidly to gossip, it isn't your natural way to be unkind, caustic or backbiting. As a result it would seem that you have all the prerequisites to live an extremely happy life. Alas, things are rarely quite that easy.

It is very important for you to demonstrate to yourself, as well as to others, that you are an individual with thoughts and feelings of your own. So often do you defer to the needs of those around you that the real you gets somewhat squashed on the way. There have to be times when you are willing to say 'yes' or 'no' unequivocally, instead of a noncommittal 'I don't really mind' or 'whatever you think best'. At the end of the day you do have opinions and can lead yourself into the path of some severe frustrations if you are unwilling to voice them in the first place.

Try to be particularly honest in deep, emotional attachments. Many Libran relationships come to grief simply because there isn't enough earthy honesty present in the first place. People knowing how you feel won't make them care for you any less. A fully integrated, truthful Libran, with a willingness to participate in the decision making, turns out to be the person who is both successful and happy.

LIBRA ON THE CUSP

Old Moore is often asked how astrological profiles are altered for those people born at either the beginning or the end of a zodiac sign, or, more properly, on the cusps of a sign. In the case of Libra this would be on the 24th of September and for two or three days after, and similarly at the end of the sign, probably from the 21st to the 23rd of October. In this year's Astral Diaries, once again, Old Moore sets out to explain the differences regarding cuspid signs.

The Virgo Cusp – September 24th to 26th

Here we find a Libran subject with a greater than average sense of responsibility and probably a better potential for success than is usually the case for Libra when taken alone. The Virgoan tendency to take itself rather too seriously is far less likely when the sign is mixed with Libra and the resultant nature is often deeply inspiring, and yet quite centred. The Virgo-cusp Libran has what it takes to break through the red tape of society, and yet can understand the need for its existence in the first place. You are caring and concerned, quick on the uptake and very ready to listen to any point of view but, at the end of the day, you know when it is going to be necessary to take a personal stance and this you are far more willing to do than would be the case for non-cuspid Librans.

Family members are important to you, but you always allow them their own individuality and won't get in the way of their personal need to spread their own wings, even at times when it's hard to take this positive stance. Practically speaking, you are a good home-maker but you also enjoy travelling and can benefit greatly from seeing the way other cultures think and behave. It is true that you can have the single- mindedness of a Virgoan, but even this aspect is modified by the Libran within you, so that you usually try to see alternative points of view and often succeed in doing so.

At work you really come into your own. Not only are you capable enough to deal with just about any eventuality, you are also willing to be flexible and to make up your mind instantly when it proves necessary to do so. Colleagues and subordinates alike tend to trust you. You may consider self-employment, unlike most Librans who are usually very worried by this prospect. Making your way in life is something you tend to take for granted, even when the going gets tough.

What people most like about you is that, despite your tremendously practical approach to life, you can be very zany and retain a sense of fun that is, at its best, second to none. Few people find you difficult to understand or to get on with in a day-to-day sense.

The Scorpio Cusp – October 21st to 23rd

The main difference between this cusp and the one at the Virgo end of Libra, is that you tend to be more emotionally motivated and of a slightly less practical nature. Routines are easy for you to address, though you can become very restless and tend to find your own emotional responses difficult to deal with. Sometimes even you don't understand what makes you tick, and that can be a problem. Actually you are not as complicated as you may have come to believe. It's simply that you have a unique view of life and one that doesn't always match that of the people around you, but as Libra instinctively wants to conform, this can lead to some personal confusion.

In family matters you are responsible, very caring and deeply committed to others. It's probable that you work in some field that finds you in direct contact with the public at large and many Scorpio-cusp Librans choose welfare, social or hospital work as a first choice. When it comes to love, you are flexible in your choice and the necessary attributes to promote a long-lasting and happy relationship are clearly present in your basic nature. If there are problems, they may come about as a result of your inability to choose properly in the first place, because you are the first to offer anyone the benefit of the doubt.

When it comes to the practicalities of life, Scorpio can prove to be extremely useful. It offers an 'edge' to your nature and, as Scorpio is a Fixed sign, you are less likely to lose ground because of lack of confidence than Libra alone would be. Your future can be bright, but only if you are willing to get involved in something that really interests you in the first place. You certainly do not care for getting your hands dirty and tend to gravitate towards more refined positions.

Creative potential is good and you could be very artistic, though if this extends to fine art, at least some of your pictures will have 'dark' overtones that might shock some people, including yourself. At base you are kind, caring, complicated, yet inspiring.

LIBRA AND ITS ASCENDANTS

The nature of every individual on the planet is composed of the rich variety of zodiac signs and planetary positions that were present at the time of their birth. Your Sun sign, which in your case is Libra, is one of the many factors when it comes to assessing the unique person you are. Probably the most important consideration, other than your Sun sign, is to establish the zodiac sign that was rising over the eastern horizon at the time that you were born. This is your Ascending or Rising sign. Most popular astrology fails to take account of the Ascendant, and yet its importance remains with you from the very moment of your birth, through every day of your life. The Ascendant is evident in the way you approach the world, and so, when meeting a person for the first time, it is this astrological influence that you are most likely to notice first. Our Ascending sign essentially represents what we appear to be, while the Sun sign is what we feel inside ourselves.

The Ascendant also has the potential for modifying our overall nature. For example, if you were born at a time of day when Libra was passing over the eastern horizon (this would be around the time of dawn) then you would be classed as a double Libran. As such, you would typify this zodiac sign, both internally and in your dealings with others. However, if your Ascendant sign turned out to be a Water sign, such as Pisces, there would be a profound alteration of nature, away from the expected qualities of Libra.

One of the reasons why popular astrology often ignores the Ascendant is that it has always been rather difficult to establish. Old Moore has found a way to make this possible by devising an easy-to-use table, which you will find on page 158 of this book. Using this, you can establish your Ascendant sign at a glance. You will need to know your rough time of birth, then it is simply a case of following the instructions.

For those readers who have no idea of their time of birth it might be worth allowing a good friend, or perhaps your partner, to read through the section that follows this introduction. Someone who deals with you on a regular basis may easily discover your Ascending sign, even though you could have some difficulty establishing it for yourself. A good understanding of this component of your nature is essential if you want to be aware of that 'other person' who is responsible for the way you make contact with the world at large. Your Sun sign, Ascendant sign, and the other pointers in this book will, together, allow you a far better understanding of what makes you tick as an individual. Peeling back the different layers of your astrological make-up can be an enlightening experience, and the Ascendant may represent one of the most important layers of all.

Libra with Libra Ascendant

There is no doubt that you carry the very best of all Libran worlds in your nature, though at the same time there is a definite possibility that you often fall between two stools. The literal advice as a result is that you must sometimes make a decision, even though it isn't all that easy for you to do so. Not everyone understands your easy-going side and there are occasions when you could appear to be too flippant for your own good. The way you approach the world makes you popular, and there is no doubt at all that you are the most diplomatic person to be found anywhere in the length and breadth of the zodiac. It is your job in life to stop people disagreeing and since you can always see every point of view, you make a good impression on the way.

Relationships can sometimes be awkward for you because you can change your mind so easily. But love is never lacking and you can be fairly certain of a generally happy life. Over-indulging is always a potential problem for Air-sign people such as yourself, and there are times in your life when you must get the rest and relaxation which is so important in funding a strong nervous system. Drink plenty of water to flush out a system that can be over-high in natural salts.

Libra with Scorpio Ascendant

There is some tendency for you to be far more deep than the average Libran would appear to be, and for this reason it is crucial that you lighten up from time to time. Every person with a Scorpio quality needs to remember that there is a happy and carefree side to all events, and your Libran quality should allow you to bear this in mind. Sometimes you try to do too many things at the same time. This is fine if you take the casual overview of Libra, but less sensible when you insist on picking the last bone out of every potential, as is much more the case for Scorpio.

When worries come along, as they sometimes will, be able to listen to what your friends have to say and also realise that they are more than willing to work on your behalf, if only because you are so loyal to them. You do have a quality of self-deception, but this should not get in the way too much if you combine the instinctive actions of Libra with the deep intuition of your Scorpio component.

Probably the most important factor of this combination is your ability to succeed in a financial sense. You make a good manager, but not of the authoritarian sort. Jobs in the media or where you are expected to make up your mind quickly would suit you because there is always an underpinning of practical sense that rarely lets you down.

Libra with Sagittarius Ascendant

A very happy combination this, with a great desire for life in all its forms and a need to push forward the bounds of the possible in a way that few other zodiac sign connections would do. You don't like the unpleasant or ugly in life and yet you are capable of dealing with both if you have to. Giving so much to humanity, you still manage to retain a degree of individuality that would surprise many, charm others, and please all.

On the reverse side of the same coin you might find that you are sometimes accused of being fickle, but this is only an expression of your need for change and variety, which is endemic to both these signs. True, you have more of a temper than would be the case for Libra when taken on its own, but such incidents would see you up and down in a flash, and it is almost impossible for you to bear a grudge of any sort. Routines get on your nerves and you are far happier when you can please yourself and get ahead at your own pace, which is quite fast.

As a lover you can make a big impression and most of you will not go short of affection in the early days, before you choose to commit yourself. Once you do, there is always a chance of romantic problems, but these are less likely when you have chosen carefully in the first place.

Libra with Capricorn Ascendant

It is a fact that Libra is the most patient of the Air signs, though like the others it needs to get things done fairly quickly. Capricorn, on the other hand, will work long and hard to achieve its objectives and will not be thwarted in the end. As a result this is a quite powerful sign combination and one that should lead to ultimate success.

Capricorn is often accused of taking itself too seriously and yet it has an ironic and really very funny sense of humour which only its chief confidants recognise. Libra is lighthearted, always willing to have fun and quite anxious to please. When these two basic types come together in their best forms, you might find yourself to be one of the most well-balanced people around. Certainly you know what you want, but you don't have to use a bulldozer in order to get it.

Active and enthusiastic when something really takes your fancy, you might also turn out to be one of the very best lovers of them all. The reason for this is that you have the depth of Capricorn but the lighter and more directly affectionate qualities of the Scales. What you want from life in a personal sense, you eventually tend to get, but you don't care too much if this takes you a while. Few people could deny that you are a faithful friend, a happy sort and a deeply magnetic personality.

Libra with Aquarius Ascendant

Stand by for a truly interesting and very inspiring combination here, but one that is sometimes rather difficult to fathom, even for the sort of people who believe themselves to be very perceptive. The reason for this could be that any situation has to be essentially fixed and constant in order to get a handle on it, and this is certainly not the case for the Aquarian–Libran type. The fact is that both these signs are Air signs, and to a certain extent as unpredictable as the wind itself.

To most people you seem to be original, frank, free and very outspoken. Not everything you do makes sense to others, and if you were alive during the hippy era, it is likely that you went around with flowers in your hair, for you are a free-thinking idealist at heart. With age you mature somewhat, but never too much, because you will always see the strange, the comical and the original in life. This is what keeps you young and is one of the factors that makes you so very attractive to members of the opposite sex. Many people will want to 'adopt' you, and you are at your very best when in company.

Much of your effort is expounded on others and yet, unless you discipline yourself a good deal, personal relationships of the romantic sort can bring certain difficulties. Careful planning is necessary.

Libra with Pisces Ascendant

An Air and Water combination, you are not easy to understand and have depths that show at times, surprising those people who thought they already knew what you were. You will always keep people guessing and are just as likely to hitchhike around Europe as you are to hold down a steady job, both of which you would undertake with the same degree of commitment and success. Usually young at heart, but always carrying the potential for an old head on young shoulders, you are something of a paradox and not at all easy for totally 'straight' types to understand. But you always make an impression and tend to be very attractive to members of the opposite sex.

In matters of health you do have to be a little careful because you dissipate much nervous energy and can sometimes be inclined to push yourself too hard, at least in a mental sense. Frequent periods of rest and meditation will do you the world of good and should improve your level of wisdom, which tends to be fairly high already. Much of your effort in life is expounded on behalf of humanity as a whole, for you care deeply, love totally and always give of your best. Whatever your faults and failings might be, you are one of the most popular people around.

Libra with Aries Ascendant

Libra has the tendency to bring out the best in any zodiac sign, and this is no exception when it comes together with Aries. You may, in fact, be the most comfortable of all Aries types, simply because Libra tempers some of your more assertive qualities and gives you the chance to balance out opposing forces, both inside yourself and in the world outside. You are fun to be with and make the staunchest friend possible. Although you are generally affable, few people would try to put one over on you because they would quickly come to know how far you are willing to go before you let forth a string of invective that would shock those who previously underestimated your basic Aries traits.

Home and family are very dear to you, but you are more tolerant than some Aries types are inclined to be and you have a youthful zest for life that should stay with you no matter what age you manage to achieve. There is always something interesting to do and your mind is a constant stream of possibilities. This makes you very creative and you may also demonstrate a desire to look good at all times. You may not always be quite as confident as you appear to be, but few would guess the fact.

Libra with Taurus Ascendant

A fortunate combination in many ways, this is a double-Venus rulership, since both Taurus and Libra are heavily reliant on the planet of love. You are social, amiable and a natural diplomat, anxious to please and ready to care for just about anyone who shows interest in you. You hate disorder, which means that there is a place for everything and everything in its place. This can throw up the odd paradox however, since being half Libran you cannot always work out where that place ought to be! You deal with life in a humorous way and are quite capable of seeing the absurd in yourself, as well as in others. Your heart is no bigger than that of the quite typical Taurean, but it sits rather closer to the surface and so others recognise it more.

On those occasions when you know you are standing on firm ground you can show great confidence, even if you have to be ready to change some of your opinions at the drop of a hat. When this happens you can be quite at odds with yourself, because Taurus doesn't take very many U-turns, whereas Libra does. Don't expect to know yourself too well, and keep looking for the funny side of things, because it is within humour that you forge the sort of life that suits you best.

Libra with Gemini Ascendant

What a happy-go-lucky soul you are and how popular you tend to be with those around you. Libra is, like Gemini, an Air sign and this means that you are the communicator par excellence, even by Gemini standards. It can sometimes be difficult for you to make up your mind about things because Libra does not exactly aid this process, and especially not when it is allied to Mercurial Gemini. Frequent periods of deep thought are necessary, and meditation would do you a great deal of good. All the same, although you might sometimes be rather unsure of yourself, you are rarely without a certain balance. Clean and tidy surroundings suit you the best, though this is far from easy to achieve because you are invariably dashing off to some place or other, so you really need someone to sort things out in your absence.

The most important fact of all is that you are much loved by your friends, of which there are likely to be very many. Because you are so willing to help them out, in return they are usually there when it matters and they would probably go to almost any length on your behalf. You exhibit a fine sense of justice and will usually back those in trouble. Charities tend to be attractive to you and you do much on behalf of those who live on the fringes of society or people who are truly alone.

Libra with Cancer Ascendant

What an absolutely pleasant and approachable sort of person you are, and how much you have to offer. Like most people associated with the sign of Cancer you give yourself freely to the world, and will always be on hand if anyone is in trouble or needs the special touch you can bring to almost any problem. Behaving in this way is the biggest part of what you are and so people come to rely on you very heavily. Like Libra you can see both sides of any coin and you exhibit the Libran tendency to jump about from one foot to the other when it is necessary to make decisions relating to your own life. This is not usually the case when you are dealing with others however, because the cooler and more detached qualities of Cancer will show through in these circumstances.

It would be fair to say that you do not deal with routines as well as Cancer alone might do and you need a degree of variety in your life, which in your case often comes in the form of travel, which can be distant and of long duration. It isn't unusual for people who have this zodiac combination to end up living abroad, though even this does little to prevent you from getting itchy feet from time to time. In romance you show an original quality that keeps the relationship young and working very well.

Libra with Leo Ascendant

Libra brings slightly more flexibility to the fixed quality of the Leo nature. On the whole you do not represent a picture that is so much different from other versions of the Lion, though you find more time to smile, enjoy changing your mind a great deal more and have a greater number of casual friends. Few would find you proud or haughty and you retain the common touch that can be so important when it comes to getting on in life generally. At work you like to do something that brings variety, and would probably soon tire of doing the same task over and over again. Many of you are teachers, for you have patience, allied to a stubborn core. This can be an indispensable combination on occasions and is part of the reason for the material success that many folk with this combination of signs achieve.

It isn't often that you get down in the dumps, after all there is generally something more important around the next corner, and you love the cut and thrust of everyday life. You always manage to stay young at heart, no matter what your age might be, and you revel in the company of interesting and stimulating types. Maybe you should try harder to concentrate on one thing at once and also strive to retain a serious opinion for more than ten minutes at a time. However, Leo helps to control your flighty tendencies.

Libra with Virgo Ascendant

Libra has the ability to lighten almost any load, and it is particularly good at doing so when it is brought together with the much more repressed sign of Virgo. To the world at large you seem relaxed, happy and able to cope with most of the pressures that life places upon you. Not only do you deal with your own life in a bright and breezy manner but you are usually on hand to help others out of any dilemma that they might make for themselves. With excellent powers of communication, you leave the world at large in no doubt whatsoever concerning both your opinions and your wishes. It is in the talking stakes that you really excel because Virgo brings the silver tongue of Mercury and Libra adds the Air-sign desire to be in constant touch with the world outside your door.

You like to have a good time and can often be found in the company of interesting and stimulating people, who have the ability to bring out the very best in your bright and sparkling personality. Underneath however, there is still much of the worrying Virgoan to be found and this means that you have to learn to relax inside as well as appearing to do so externally. In fact you are much more complex than most people would realise, and definitely would not be suited to a life that allowed you too much time to think about yourself.

THE MOON AND THE PART IT PLAYS IN YOUR LIFE

In astrology the Moon is probably the single most important heavenly body after the Sun. Its unique position, as partner to the Earth on its journey around the solar system, means that the Moon appears to pass through the signs of the zodiac extremely quickly. The zodiac position of the Moon at the time of your birth plays a great part in personal character and is especially significant in the build-up of your emotional nature.

Sun Moon Cycles

The first lunar cycle deals with the part the position of the Moon plays relative to your Sun sign. I have made the fluctuations of this pattern easy for you to understand by means of a simple cyclic graph. It appears on the first page of each 'Your Month At A Glance', under the title 'Highs and Lows'. The graph displays the lunar cycle and you will soon learn to understand how its movements have a bearing on your level of energy and your abilities.

Your Own Moon Sign

Discovering the position of the Moon at the time of your birth has always been notoriously difficult because tracking the complex zodiac positions of the Moon is not easy. This process has been reduced to three simple stages with Old Moore's unique Lunar Tables. A breakdown of the Moon's zodiac positions can be found from page 25 onwards, so that once you know what your Moon Sign is, you can see what part this plays in the overall build-up of your personal character.

If you follow the instructions on the next page you will soon be able to work out exactly what zodiac sign the Moon occupied on the day that you were born and you can then go on to compare the reading for this position with those of your Sun sign and your Ascendant. It is partly the comparison between these three important positions that goes towards making you the unique individual you are.

HOW TO DISCOVER YOUR MOON SIGN

This is a three-stage process. You may need a pen and a piece of paper but if you follow the instructions below the process should only take a minute or so.

STAGE 1 First of all you need to know the Moon Age at the time of your birth. If you look at Moon Table 1, on page 23, you will find all the years between 1915 and 2013 down the left side. Find the year of your birth and then trace across to the right to the month of your birth. Where the two intersect you will find a number. This is the date of the New Moon in the month that you were born. You now need to count forward the number of days between the New Moon and your own birthday. For example, if the New Moon in the month of your birth was shown as being the 6th and you were born on the 20th, your Moon Age Day would be 14. If the New Moon in the month of your birth came after your birthday, you need to count forward from the New Moon in the previous month. Whatever the result, jot this number down so that you do not forget it.

STAGE 2 Take a look at Moon Table 2 on page 24. Down the left hand column look for the date of your birth. Now trace across to the month of your birth. Where the two meet you will find a letter. Copy this letter down alongside your Moon Age Day.

STAGE 3 Moon Table 3 on page 24 will supply you with the zodiac sign the Moon occupied on the day of your birth. Look for your Moon Age Day down the left hand column and then for the letter you found in Stage 2. Where the two converge you will find a zodiac sign and this is the sign occupied by the Moon on the day that you were born.

Your Zodiac Moon Sign Explained

You will find a profile of all zodiac Moon Signs on pages 25 to 28, showing in yet another way how astrology helps to make you into the individual that you are. In each daily entry of the Astral Diary you can find the zodiac position of the Moon for every day of the year. This also allows you to discover your lunar birthdays. Since the Moon passes through all the signs of the zodiac in about a month, you can expect something like twelve lunar birthdays each year. At these times you are likely to be emotionally steady and able to make the sort of decisions that have real, lasting value.

MOON TABLE 1

YEAR	AUG	SEP	OCT	YEAR	AUG	SEP	OCT	YEAR	AUG	SEP	OCT
1915	10	9	8	1948	5	3	2	1981	29	28	27
1916	29	27	27	1949	24	23	21	1982	19	17	17
1917	17	15	15	1950	13	12	11	1983	8	7	6
1918	6	4	4	1951	2	1	1/30	1984	26	25	24
1919	25	23	23	1952	20	19	18	1985	16	14	14
1920	14	12	12	1953	9	8	8	1986	5	4	3
1921	3	2	1/30	1954	28	27	26	1987	24	23	22
1922	22	21	20	1955	17	16	15	1988	12	11	10
1923	12	10	10	1956	6	4	4	1989	1/31	29	29
1924	30	28	28	1957	25	23	23	1990	20	19	18
1925	19	18	17	1958	15	13	12	1991	9	8	8
1926	8	7	6	1959	4	3	2/31	1992	28	26	25
1927	27	25	25	1960	22	21	20	1993	17	16	15
1928	16	14	14	1961	11	10	9	1994	7	5	5
1929	5	3	2	1962	30	28	28	1995	26	24	24
1930	24	22	20	1963	19	17	17	1996	14	13	11
1931	13	12	11	1964	7	6	5	1997	3	2	2/31
1932	2/31	30	29	1965	26	25	24	1998	22	20	20
1933	21	19	19	1966	16	14	14	1999	11	10	8
1934	10	9	8	1967	5	4	3	2000	29	27	27
1935	29	27	27	1968	24	23	22	2001	19	17	17
1936	17	15	15	1969	12	11	10	2002	8	6	6
1937	6	4	4	1970	2	1	1/30	2003	27	26	25
1938	25	23	23	1971	20	19	19	2004	14	13	12
1939	15	13	12	1972	9	8	8	2005	4	3	2
1940	4	2	1/30	1973	28	27	26	2006	23	22	21
1941	22	21	20	1974	17	16	15	2007	13	12	11
1942	12	10	10	1975	7	5	5	2008	1/31	30	29
1943	1/30	29	29	1976	25	23	23	2009	20	19	18
1944	18	17	17	1977	14	13	12	2010	10	8	8
1945	8	6	6	1978	4	2	2/31	2011	29	27	27
1946	26	25	24	1979	22	21	20	2012	17	16	15
1947	16	14	14	1980	11	10	9	2013	6	4	4

TABLE 2

DAY	SEP	OCT
1	X	a
2	X	a
3	X	a
4	Y	b
5	Y	b
6	Y	b
7	Y	b
8	Y	b
9	Y	b
10	Y	b
11	Y	b
12	Y	b
13	Y	b
14	Z	d
15	Z	d
16	Z	d
17	Z	d
18	Z	d
19	Z	d
20	Z	d
21	Z	d
22	Z	d
23	Z	d
24	a	e
25	a	e
26	a	e
27	a	e
28	a	e
29	a	e
30	a	e
31	–	e

TABLE 3

M/D	X	Y	Z	a	b	d	e
0	VI	VI	LI	LI	LI	LI	SC
1	VI	LI	LI	LI	LI	SC	SC
2	LI	LI	LI	LI	SC	SC	SC
3	LI	LI	SC	SC	SC	SC	SA
4	LI	SC	SC	SC	SA	SA	SA
5	SC	SC	SC	SA	SA	SA	CP
6	SC	SA	SA	SA	CP	CP	CP
7	SA	SA	SA	SA	CP	CP	AQ
8	SA	SA	CP	CP	CP	CP	AQ
9	SA	CP	CP	CP	AQ	AQ	AQ
10	CP	CP	CP	AQ	AQ	AQ	PI
11	CP	AQ	AQ	AQ	PI	PI	PI
12	AQ	AQ	AQ	PI	PI	PI	AR
13	AQ	AQ	PI	PI	AR	PI	AR
14	PI	PI	PI	AR	AR	AR	TA
15	PI	PI	PI	AR	AR	AR	TA
16	PI	AR	AR	AR	AR	TA	TA
17	AR	AR	AR	AR	TA	TA	GE
18	AR	AR	AR	TA	TA	GE	GE
19	AR	TA	TA	TA	TA	GE	GE
20	TA	TA	TA	GE	GE	GE	CA
21	TA	GE	GE	GE	GE	CA	CA
22	GE	GE	GE	GE	CA	CA	CA
23	GE	GE	GE	CA	CA	CA	LE
24	GE	CA	CA	CA	CA	LE	LE
25	CA	CA	CA	CA	LE	LE	LE
26	CA	LE	LE	LE	LE	VI	VI
27	LE	LE	LE	LE	VI	VI	VI
28	LE	LE	LE	VI	VI	VI	LI
29	LE	VI	VI	VI	VI	LI	LI

AR = Aries, TA = Taurus, GE = Gemini, CA = Cancer, LE = Leo, VI = Virgo, LI = Libra, SC = Scorpio, SA = Sagittarius, CP = Capricorn, AQ = Aquarius, PI = Pisces

MOON SIGNS

Moon in Aries

You have a strong imagination, courage, determination and a desire to do things in your own way and forge your own path through life.

Originality is a key attribute; you are seldom stuck for ideas although your mind is changeable and you could take the time to focus on individual tasks. Often quick-tempered, you take orders from few people and live life at a fast pace. Avoid health problems by taking regular time out for rest and relaxation.

Emotionally, it is important that you talk to those you are closest to and work out your true feelings. Once you discover that people are there to help, there is less necessity for you to do everything yourself.

Moon in Taurus

The Moon in Taurus gives you a courteous and friendly manner, which means you are likely to have many friends.

The good things in life mean a lot to you, as Taurus is an Earth sign that delights in experiences which please the senses. Hence you are probably a lover of good food and drink, which may in turn mean you need to keep an eye on the bathroom scales, especially as looking good is also important to you.

Emotionally you are fairly stable and you stick by your own standards. Taureans do not respond well to change. Intuition also plays an important part in your life.

Moon in Gemini

You have a warm-hearted character, sympathetic and eager to help others. At times reserved, you can also be articulate and chatty: this is part of the paradox of Gemini, which always brings duplicity to the nature. You are interested in current affairs, have a good intellect, and are good company and likely to have many friends. Most of your friends have a high opinion of you and would be ready to defend you should the need arise. However, this is usually unnecessary, as you are quite capable of defending yourself in any verbal confrontation.

Travel is important to your inquisitive mind and you find intellectual stimulus in mixing with people from different cultures. You also gain much from reading, writing and the arts but you do need plenty of rest and relaxation in order to avoid fatigue.

Moon in Cancer

The Moon in Cancer at the time of birth is a fortunate position as Cancer is the Moon's natural home. This means that the qualities of compassion and understanding given by the Moon are especially enhanced in your nature, and you are friendly and sociable and cope well with emotional pressures. You cherish home and family life, and happily do the domestic tasks. Your surroundings are important to you and you hate squalor and filth. You are likely to have a love of music and poetry.

Your basic character, although at times changeable like the Moon itself, depends on symmetry. You aim to make your surroundings comfortable and harmonious, for yourself and those close to you.

Moon in Leo

The best qualities of the Moon and Leo come together to make you warmhearted, fair, ambitious and self-confident. With good organisational abilities, you invariably rise to a position of responsibility in your chosen career. This is fortunate as you don't enjoy being an 'also-ran' and would rather be an important part of a small organisation than a menial in a large one.

You should be lucky in love, and happy, provided you put in the effort to make a comfortable home for yourself and those close to you. It is likely that you will have a love of pleasure, sport, music and literature. Life brings you many rewards, most of them as a direct result of your own efforts, although you may be luckier than average and ready to make the best of any situation.

Moon in Virgo

You are endowed with good mental abilities and a keen receptive memory, but you are never ostentatious or pretentious. Naturally quite reserved, you still have many friends, especially of the opposite sex. Marital relationships must be discussed carefully and worked at so that they remain harmonious, as personal attachments can be a problem if you do not give them your full attention.

Talented and persevering, you possess artistic qualities and are a good homemaker. Earning your honours through genuine merit, you work long and hard towards your objectives but show little pride in your achievements. Many short journeys will be undertaken in your life.

Moon in Libra

With the Moon in Libra you are naturally popular and make friends easily. People like you, probably more than you realise, you bring fun to a party and are a natural diplomat. For all its good points, Libra is not the most stable of astrological signs and, as a result, your emotions can be a little unstable too. Therefore, although the Moon in Libra is said to be good for love and marriage, your Sun sign and Rising sign will have an important effect on your emotional and loving qualities.

You must remember to relate to others in your decision-making. Co-operation is crucial because Libra represents the 'balance' of life that can only be achieved through harmonious relationships. Conformity is not easy for you because Libra, an Air sign, likes its independence.

Moon in Scorpio

Some people might call you pushy. In fact, all you really want to do is to live life to the full and protect yourself and your family from the pressures of life. Take care to avoid giving the impression of being sarcastic or impulsive and use your energies wisely and constructively.

You have great courage and you invariably achieve your goals by force of personality and sheer effort. You are fond of mystery and are good at predicting the outcome of situations and events. Travel experiences can be beneficial to you.

You may experience problems if you do not take time to examine your motives in a relationship, and also if you allow jealousy, always a feature of Scorpio, to cloud your judgement.

Moon in Sagittarius

The Moon in Sagittarius helps to make you a generous individual with humanitarian qualities and a kind heart. Restlessness may be intrinsic as your mind is seldom still. Perhaps because of this, you have a need for change that could lead you to several major moves during your adult life. You are not afraid to stand your ground when you know your judgement is right, you speak directly and have good intuition.

At work you are quick, efficient and versatile and so you make an ideal employee. You need work to be intellectually demanding and do not enjoy tedious routines.

In relationships, you anger quickly if faced with stupidity or deception, though you are just as quick to forgive and forget. Emotionally, there are times when your heart rules your head.

Moon in Capricorn

The Moon in Capricorn makes you popular and likely to come into the public eye in some way. The watery Moon is not entirely comfortable in the Earth sign of Capricorn and this may lead to some difficulties in the early years of life. An initial lack of creative ability and indecision must be overcome before the true qualities of patience and perseverance inherent in Capricorn can show through.

You have good administrative ability and are a capable worker, and if you are careful you can accumulate wealth. But you must be cautious and take professional advice in partnerships, as you are open to deception. You may be interested in social or welfare work, which suit your organisational skills and sympathy for others.

Moon in Aquarius

The Moon in Aquarius makes you an active and agreeable person with a friendly, easy-going nature. Sympathetic to the needs of others, you flourish in a laid-back atmosphere. You are broad-minded, fair and open to suggestion, although sometimes you have an unconventional quality which others can find hard to understand.

You are interested in the strange and curious, and in old articles and places. You enjoy trips to these places and gain much from them. Political, scientific and educational work interests you and you might choose a career in science or technology.

Money-wise, you make gains through innovation and concentration and Lunar Aquarians often tackle more than one job at a time. In love you are kind and honest.

Moon in Pisces

You have a kind, sympathetic nature, somewhat retiring at times, but you always take account of others' feelings and help when you can.

Personal relationships may be problematic, but as life goes on you can learn from your experiences and develop a better understanding of yourself and the world around you.

You have a fondness for travel, appreciate beauty and harmony and hate disorder and strife. You may be fond of literature and would make a good writer or speaker yourself. You have a creative imagination and may come across as an incurable romantic. You have strong intuition, maybe bordering on a mediumistic quality, which sets you apart from the mass. You may not be rich in cash terms, but your personal gifts are worth more than gold.

LIBRA IN LOVE

Discover how compatible you are with people from the same and other signs of the zodiac. Five stars equals a match made in heaven!

Libra meets Libra

This is a potentially successful match because Librans are extremely likeable people, and so it stands to reason that two Librans together will be twice as pleasant and twice as much fun. However, Librans can also be indecisive and need an anchor from which to find practical and financial success, and obviously one Libran won't provide this for another. Librans can be flighty in a romantic sense, so both parties will need to develop a steadfast approach for a long-term relationship. Star rating: ****

Libra meets Scorpio

Many astrologers have reservations about this match because, on the surface, the signs are so different. However, this couple may find fulfilment because these differences mean that their respective needs are met. Scorpio needs a partner to lighten the load which won't daunt Libra, while Libra looks for a steadfast quality which it doesn't possess, but Scorpio can supply naturally. Financial success is possible because they both have good ideas and back them up with hard work and determination. All in all, a promising outlook. Star rating: ****

Libra meets Sagittarius

Libra and Sagittarius are both adaptable signs who get on well with most people, but this promising outlook often does not follow through because each brings out the flighty side of the other. This combination is great for a fling, but when the romance is over someone needs to see to the practical side of life. Both signs are well meaning, pleasant and kind, but are either of them constant enough to build a life together? In at least some of the cases, the answer would be no. Star rating: ***

Libra meets Capricorn

Libra and Capricorn rub each other up the wrong way because their attitudes to life are so different, and although both are capable of doing something about this, in reality they probably won't. Capricorn is steady, determined and solid, while Libra is bright but sometimes superficial and not entirely reliable. They usually lack the instant spark needed to get them together in the first place, so when it does happen it is often because one of the partners is not typical of their sign. Star rating: **

Libra meets Aquarius

One of the best combinations imaginable, partly because both are Air signs and so share a common meeting point. But perhaps the more crucial factor is that both signs respect each other. Aquarius loves life and originality, and is quite intellectual. Libra is similar, but more balanced and rather less eccentric. A visit to this couple's house would be entertaining and full of zany wit, activity and excitement. Both are keen to travel and may prefer to 'find themselves' before taking on too many domestic responsibilities. Star rating: *****

Libra meets Pisces

Libra and Pisces can be extremely fond of each other, even deeply in love, but this alone isn't a stable foundation for long-term success. Pisces is extremely deep and doesn't even know itself very well. Libra may initially find this intriguing but will eventually feel frustrated at being unable to understand the Piscean's emotional and personal feelings. Pisces can be jealous and may find Libra's flightiness difficult, which Libra can't stand. They are great friends and they may make it to the romantic stakes, but when they get there a lot of effort will be necessary. Star rating: ***

Libra meets Aries

These are zodiac opposites which means a make-or-break situation. The match will either be a great success or a dismal failure. Why? Well, Aries finds it difficult to understand the flighty Air-sign tendencies of Libra, whilst the natural balance of Libra contradicts the unorthodox Arian methods. Any flexibility will come from Libra, which may mean that things work out for a while, but Libra only has so much patience and it may eventually run out. In the end, Aries may be just too bossy for an independent but sensitive sign like Libra. Star rating: **

Libra meets Taurus

A happy life is important to both these signs and, as they are both ruled by Venus, they share a common understanding, even though they display themselves so differently. Taurus is quieter than Libra, but can be decisive, and that's what counts. Libra is interested in absolutely everything, an infectious quality when seen through Taurean eyes. The slightly flighty qualities of Libra may lead to jealousy from the Bull. Not an argumentative relationship and one that often works well. There could be many changes of address for this pair. Star rating: ****

Libra meets Gemini

One of the best possible zodiac combinations. Libra and Gemini are both Air signs, which leads to a meeting of minds. Both signs simply love to have a good time, although Libra is the tidiest and less forgetful. Gemini's capricious nature won't bother Libra, who acts as a stabilising influence. Life should generally run smoothly, and any rows are likely to be short and sharp. Both parties genuinely like each other, which is of paramount importance in a relationship and, ultimately, there isn't a better reason for being or staying together. Star rating: *****

Libra meets Cancer

Almost anyone can get on with Libra, which is one of the most adaptable signs of them all. But being adaptable does not always lead to fulfilment and a successful match here will require a quiet Libran and a slightly more progressive Cancerian than the norm. Both signs are pleasant and polite, and like domestic order, but Libra may find Cancer too emotional and perhaps lacking in vibrancy, while Libra, on the other hand, may be a little too flighty for steady Cancer. Star rating: ***

Libra meets Leo

The biggest drawback here is likely to be in the issue of commitment. Leo knows everything about constancy and faithfulness, a lesson which, sadly, Libra needs to learn. Librans are easy-going and diplomatic, qualities which are useful when Leo is on the war-path. This couple should be compatible on a personal level and any problems tend to relate to the different way in which these signs deal with outside factors. With good will and an open mind, it can work out well enough. Star rating: ***

Libra meets Virgo

There have been some rare occasions when this match has found great success, but usually the darker and more inward-looking Virgoan depresses the naturally gregarious Libran. Libra appears self-confident, but is not so beneath the surface, and needs encouragement to develop inner confidence, which may not come from Virgo. Constancy can be a problem for Libra, who also tires easily and may find Virgo dull. A lighter, less serious approach to life from Virgo is needed to make this work. Star rating: **

VENUS:
THE PLANET OF LOVE

If you look up at the sky around sunset or sunrise you will often see Venus in close attendance to the Sun. It is arguably one of the most beautiful sights of all and there is little wonder that historically it became associated with the goddess of love. But although Venus does play an important part in the way you view love and in the way others see you romantically, this is only one of the spheres of influence that it enjoys in your overall character.

Venus has a part to play in the more cultured side of your life and has much to do with your appreciation of art, literature, music and general creativity. Even the way you look is responsive to the part of the zodiac that Venus occupied at the start of your life, though this fact is also down to your Sun sign and Ascending sign. If, at the time you were born, Venus occupied one of the more gregarious zodiac signs, you will be more likely to wear your heart on your sleeve, as well as to be more attracted to entertainment, social gatherings and good company. If on the other hand Venus occupied a quiet zodiac sign at the time of your birth, you would tend to be more retiring and less willing to shine in public situations.

It's good to know what part the planet Venus plays in your life for it can have a great bearing on the way you appear to the rest of the world and since we all have to mix with others, you can learn to make the very best of what Venus has to offer you.

One of the great complications in the past has always been trying to establish exactly what zodiac position Venus enjoyed when you were born because the planet is notoriously difficult to track. However, I have solved that problem by creating a table that is exclusive to your Sun sign, which you will find on the following page.

Establishing your Venus sign could not be easier. Just look up the year of your birth on the page opposite and you will see a sign of the zodiac. This was the sign that Venus occupied in the period covered by your sign in that year. If Venus occupied more than one sign during the period, this is indicated by the date on which the sign changed, and the name of the new sign. For instance, if you were born in 1950, Venus was in Virgo until the 4th October, after which time it was in Libra. If you were born before 4th October your Venus sign is Virgo, if you were born on or after 4th October, your Venus sign is Libra. Once you have established the position of Venus at the time of your birth, you can then look in the pages which follow to see how this has a bearing on your life as a whole.

1915 LIBRA / 16.10 SCORPIO
1916 LEO / 8.10 VIRGO
1917 SCORPIO /
   12.10 SAGITTARIUS
1918 VIRGO / 6.10 LIBRA
1919 SCORPIO /
   12.10 SAGITTARIUS
1920 LIBRA / 30.9 SCORPIO
1921 LEO / 26.9 VIRGO /
   21.10 LIBRA
1922 SCORPIO /
   11.10 SAGITTARIUS
1923 LIBRA / 16.10 SCORPIO
1924 LEO / 8.10 VIRGO
1925 SCORPIO /
   12.10 SAGITTARIUS
1926 VIRGO / 6.10 LIBRA
1927 VIRGO
1928 LIBRA / 29.9 SCORPIO
1929 LEO / 26.9 VIRGO /
   20.10 LIBRA
1930 SCORPIO /
   12.10 SAGITTARIUS
1931 LIBRA / 15.10 SCORPIO
1932 LEO / 7.10 VIRGO
1933 SCORPIO /
   11.10 SAGITTARIUS
1934 VIRGO / 5.10 LIBRA
1935 VIRGO
1936 LIBRA / 28.9 SCORPIO
1937 LEO / 25.9 VIRGO /
   20.10 LIBRA
1938 SCORPIO /
   14.10 SAGITTARIUS
1939 LIBRA / 14.10 SCORPIO
1940 LEO / 7.10 VIRGO
1941 SCORPIO /
   11.10 SAGITTARIUS
1942 VIRGO / 5.10 LIBRA
1943 VIRGO
1944 LIBRA / 28.9 SCORPIO
1945 LEO / 25.9 VIRGO /
   19.10 LIBRA
1946 SCORPIO /
   14.10 SAGITTARIUS
1947 LIBRA / 13.10 SCORPIO
1948 LEO / 7.10 VIRGO
1949 SCORPIO /
   11.10 SAGITTARIUS
1950 VIRGO / 4.10 LIBRA
1951 VIRGO
1952 LIBRA / 27.9 SCORPIO
1953 VIRGO / 19.10 LIBRA
1954 SCORPIO /
   16.10 SAGITTARIUS
1955 LIBRA / 12.10 SCORPIO
1956 LEO / 6.10 VIRGO
1957 SCORPIO /
   10.10 SAGITTARIUS
1958 VIRGO / 4.10 LIBRA

1959 VIRGO / 28.9 LEO
1960 LIBRA / 27.9 SCORPIO
1961 VIRGO / 18.10 LIBRA
1962 SCORPIO /
   16.10 SAGITTARIUS
1963 LIBRA / 12.10 SCORPIO
1964 LEO / 6.10 VIRGO
1965 SCORPIO / 9.10 SAGITTARIUS
1966 VIRGO / 4.10 LIBRA
1967 VIRGO / 3.10 LEO
1968 LIBRA / 26.9 SCORPIO
1969 VIRGO / 17.10 LIBRA
1970 SCORPIO /
   19.10 SAGITTARIUS
1971 LIBRA / 11.10 SCORPIO
1972 LEO / 6.10 VIRGO
1973 SCORPIO / 9.10 SAGITTARIUS
1974 VIRGO / 3.10 LIBRA
1975 VIRGO / 5.10 LEO
1976 LIBRA / 26.9 SCORPIO
1977 VIRGO / 17.10 LIBRA
1978 SCORPIO /
   19.10 SAGITTARIUS
1979 LIBRA / 11.10 SCORPIO
1980 LEO / 5.10 VIRGO
1981 SCORPIO / 9.10 SAGITTARIUS
1982 VIRGO / 3.10 LIBRA
1983 VIRGO / 7.10 LEO
1984 LIBRA / 25.9 SCORPIO
1985 VIRGO / 16.10 LIBRA
1986 SCORPIO
1987 LIBRA / 10.10 SCORPIO
1988 LEO / 5.10 VIRGO
1989 SCORPIO / 8.10 SAGITTARIUS
1990 VIRGO / 2.10 LIBRA
1991 VIRGO / 8.10 LEO
1992 LIBRA / 25.9 SCORPIO
1993 VIRGO / 16.10 LIBRA
1994 SCORPIO
1995 LIBRA / 10.10 SCORPIO
1996 LEO / 5.10 VIRGO
1997 SCORPIO / 8.10 SAGITTARIUS
1998 VIRGO / 2.10 LIBRA
1999 VIRGO / 9.10 LEO
2000 LIBRA / 25.9 SCORPIO
2001 LEO / 5.10 VIRGO
2002 SCORPIO / 8.10 SAGITTARIUS
2003 LIBRA / 10.10 SCORPIO
2004 LEO / 5.10 VIRGO
2005 SCORPIO / 8.10 SAGITTARIUS
2006 VIRGO / 2.10 LIBRA
2007 VIRGO / 9.10 LEO
2008 LIBRA / 25.9 SCORPIO
2009 LEO / 5.10 VIRGO
2010 SCORPIO / 8.10 SAGITTARIUS
2011 LIBRA / 10.10 SCORPIO
2012 LEO / 5.10 VIRGO
2013 SCORPIO / 8.10 SAGITTARIUS

33

VENUS THROUGH THE ZODIAC SIGNS

Venus in Aries

Amongst other things, the position of Venus in Aries indicates a fondness for travel, music and all creative pursuits. Your nature tends to be affectionate and you would try not to create confusion or difficulty for others if it could be avoided. Many people with this planetary position have a great love of the theatre, and mental stimulation is of the greatest importance. Early romantic attachments are common with Venus in Aries, so it is very important to establish a genuine sense of romantic continuity. Early marriage is not recommended, especially if it is based on sympathy. You may give your heart a little too readily on occasions.

Venus in Taurus

You are capable of very deep feelings and your emotions tend to last for a very long time. This makes you a trusting partner and lover, whose constancy is second to none. In life you are precise and careful and always try to do things the right way. Although this means an ordered life, which you are comfortable with, it can also lead you to be rather too fussy for your own good. Despite your pleasant nature, you are very fixed in your opinions and quite able to speak your mind. Others are attracted to you and historical astrologers always quoted this position of Venus as being very fortunate in terms of marriage. However, if you find yourself involved in a failed relationship, it could take you a long time to trust again.

Venus in Gemini

As with all associations related to Gemini, you tend to be quite versatile, anxious for change and intelligent in your dealings with the world at large. You may gain money from more than one source but you are equally good at spending it. There is an inference here that you are a good communicator, via either the written or the spoken word, and you love to be in the company of interesting people. Always on the look-out for culture, you may also be very fond of music, and love to indulge the curious and cultured side of your nature. In romance you tend to have more than one relationship and could find yourself associated with someone who has previously been a friend or even a distant relative.

Venus in Cancer

You often stay close to home because you are very fond of family and enjoy many of your most treasured moments when you are with those you love. Being naturally sympathetic, you will always do anything you can to support those around you, even people you hardly know at all. This charitable side of your nature is your most noticeable trait and is one of the reasons why others are naturally so fond of you. Being receptive and in some cases even psychic, you can see through to the soul of most of those with whom you come into contact. You may not commence too many romantic attachments but when you do give your heart, it tends to be unconditionally.

Venus in Leo

It must become quickly obvious to almost anyone you meet that you are kind, sympathetic and yet determined enough to stand up for anyone or anything that is truly important to you. Bright and sunny, you warm the world with your natural enthusiasm and would rarely do anything to hurt those around you, or at least not intentionally. In romance you are ardent and sincere, though some may find your style just a little overpowering. Gains come through your contacts with other people and this could be especially true with regard to romance, for love and money often come hand in hand for those who were born with Venus in Leo. People claim to understand you, though you are more complex than you seem.

Venus in Virgo

Your nature could well be fairly quiet no matter what your Sun sign might be, though this fact often manifests itself as an inner peace and would not prevent you from being basically sociable. Some delays and even the odd disappointment in love cannot be ruled out with this planetary position, though it's a fact that you will usually find the happiness you look for in the end. Catapulting yourself into romantic entanglements that you know to be rather ill-advised is not sensible, and it would be better to wait before you committed yourself exclusively to any one person. It is the essence of your nature to serve the world at large and through doing so it is possible that you will attract money at some stage in your life.

Venus in Libra

Venus is very comfortable in Libra and bestows upon those people who have this planetary position a particular sort of kindness that is easy to recognise. This is a very good position for all sorts of friendships and also for romantic attachments that usually bring much joy into your life. Few individuals with Venus in Libra would avoid marriage and since you are capable of great depths of love, it is likely that you will find a contented personal life. You like to mix with people of integrity and intelligence but don't take kindly to scruffy surroundings or work that means getting your hands too dirty. Careful speculation, good business dealings and money through marriage all seem fairly likely.

Venus in Scorpio

You are quite open and tend to spend money quite freely, even on those occasions when you don't have very much. Although your intentions are always good, there are times when you get yourself in to the odd scrape and this can be particularly true when it comes to romance, which you may come to late or from a rather unexpected direction. Certainly you have the power to be happy and to make others contented on the way, but you find the odd stumbling block on your journey through life and it could seem that you have to work harder than those around you. As a result of this, you gain a much deeper understanding of the true value of personal happiness than many people ever do, and are likely to achieve true contentment in the end.

Venus in Sagittarius

You are lighthearted, cheerful and always able to see the funny side of any situation. These facts enhance your popularity, which is especially high with members of the opposite sex. You should never have to look too far to find romantic interest in your life, though it is just possible that you might be too willing to commit yourself before you are certain that the person in question is right for you. Part of the problem here extends to other areas of life too. The fact is that you like variety in everything and so can tire of situations that fail to offer it. All the same, if you choose wisely and learn to understand your restless side, then great happiness can be yours.

Venus in Capricorn

The most notable trait that comes from Venus in this position is that it makes you trustworthy and able to take on all sorts of responsibilities in life. People are instinctively fond of you and love you all the more because you are always ready to help those who are in any form of need. Social and business popularity can be yours and there is a magnetic quality to your nature that is particularly attractive in a romantic sense. Anyone who wants a partner for a lover, a spouse and a good friend too would almost certainly look in your direction. Constancy is the hallmark of your nature and unfaithfulness would go right against the grain. You might sometimes be a little too trusting.

Venus in Aquarius

This location of Venus offers a fondness for travel and a desire to try out something new at every possible opportunity. You are extremely easy to get along with and tend to have many friends from varied backgrounds, classes and inclinations. You like to live a distinct sort of life and gain a great deal from moving about, both in a career sense and with regard to your home. It is not out of the question that you could form a romantic attachment to someone who comes from far away or be attracted to a person of a distinctly artistic and original nature. What you cannot stand is jealousy, for you have friends of both sexes and would want to keep things that way.

Venus in Pisces

The first thing people tend to notice about you is your wonderful, warm smile. Being very charitable by nature you will do anything to help others, even if you don't know them well. Much of your life may be spent sorting out situations for other people, but it is very important to feel that you are living for yourself too. In the main, you remain cheerful, and tend to be quite attractive to members of the opposite sex. Where romantic attachments are concerned, you could be drawn to people who are significantly older or younger than yourself or to someone with a unique career or point of view. It might be best for you to avoid marrying whilst you are still very young.

THE ASTRAL DIARY

HOW THE DIAGRAMS WORK

Through the picture diagrams in the Astral Diary I want to help you to plot your year. With them you can see where the positive and negative aspects will be found in each month. To make the most of them, all you have to do is remember where and when!

Let me show you how they work ...

THE MONTH AT A GLANCE

Just as there are twelve separate zodiac signs, so astrologers believe that each sign has twelve separate aspects to life. Each of the twelve segments relates to a different personal aspect. I list them all every month so that their meanings are always clear.

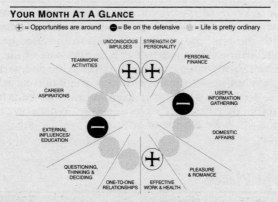

I have designed this chart to show you how and when these twelve different aspects are being influenced throughout the year. When there is a shaded circle, nothing out of the ordinary is to be expected. However, when a circle turns white with a plus sign, the influence is positive. Where the circle is black with a minus sign, it is a negative.

YOUR ENERGY RHYTHM CHART

On the opposite page is a picture diagram in which I link your zodiac group to the rhythm of the Moon. In doing this I have calculated when you will be gaining strength from its influence and equally when you may be weakened by it.

If you think of yourself as being like the tides of the ocean then you may understand how your own energies must also rise and fall. And if you understand how it works and when it is working, then you can better organise your activities to achieve more and get things done more easily.

YOUR ENERGY RHYTHM CHART
At your best on 20th–21st

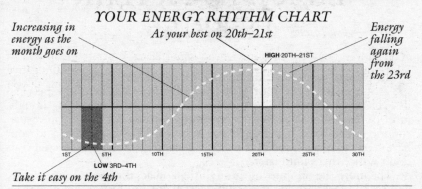

Increasing in energy as the month goes on

HIGH 20TH–21ST

Energy falling again from the 23rd

LOW 3RD–4TH

Take it easy on the 4th

MOVING PICTURE SCREEN
Love, money, career and vitality measured every week

The diagram at the end of each week is designed to be informative and fun. The arrows move up and down the scale to give you an idea of the strength of your opportunities in each area. If LOVE stands at plus 4, then get out and put yourself about because things are going your way in romance! The further down the arrow goes, the weaker the opportunities. Do note that the diagram is an overall view of your astrological aspects and therefore reflects a trend which may not concur with every day in that cycle.

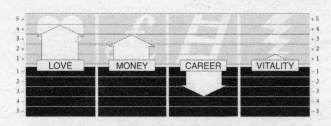

LOVE   MONEY   CAREER   VITALITY

AND FINALLY:

am..

pm ....

The two lines that are left blank in each daily entry of the Astral Diary are for your own personal use. You may find them ideal for keeping a check on birthdays or appointments, though it could also be an idea to make notes from the astrological trends and diagrams a few weeks in advance. Some of the lines are marked with a key, which indicates the working of astrological cycles in your life. Look out for them each week as they are the best days to take action or make decisions. The daily text tells you which area of your life to focus on.

☿ = Mercury is retrograde on that day.

LIBRA: YOUR YEAR
IN BRIEF

The planets' positions indicate that not everything is likely to be quite as it appears at the start of the year. During January, and especially in February, you need to be prepared for one or two surprises, though most of these should be positive in nature. Getting back into your usual routine in the New Year should not be at all difficult for you, and you have scope to make significant material gains early in the year, even if you don't notice them until later.

The more the Sun moves through the zodiac, the more comfortable you should feel with life generally. March and April offer you a chance to travel or move around and an ability to get to grips with any matters that have been hanging over since late last year. Comfort and security are issues in March, but April is more about expansive movement and new starts.

Once summer begins to paint the hedgerows you start to come into your own much more in both a material and a personal sense. The attitude of loved ones can be somewhat surprising during May and June, and you will have to make some changes in order to accommodate the sensibilities of those around you. This is a great time for love and a period when Librans who have been on their own for a while could have new opportunities to meet a partner.

July and August are potentially the busiest months of the year as far as you are concerned, and they bring a mood of compromise, as well as the chance to look in new directions. At work you are likely to be very busy and constantly in demand, whilst retired Librans, or those between jobs, could be discovering newer and interesting ways in which to fill their time. Action is forecast when it comes to travel, and one or two of your journeys could come free of charge.

In September and October the Sun moves closer to its most natural position as far as you are concerned. There ought to be more chances to prosper financially, together with less stress placed upon specific attachments. Routines are not something you will be seeking at this time because you will be entering a phase during which surprises and late decisions lift your life.

The final months of the year, November and December, ought to see you going for gold in a number of different ways. Efforts you put in earlier in the year now begin to pay dividends and you are on a pronounced and very important learning curve. Part of the reason you make gains at this time is because you are helping others – and learning a lot about yourself along the way.

♎

January
2013

YOUR MONTH AT A GLANCE

⊕ = Opportunities are around   ⊖ = Be on the defensive   ⬤ = Life is pretty ordinary

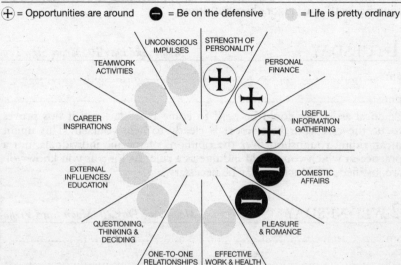

UNCONSCIOUS IMPULSES

STRENGTH OF PERSONALITY

TEAMWORK ACTIVITIES

PERSONAL FINANCE

CAREER INSPIRATIONS

USEFUL INFORMATION GATHERING

EXTERNAL INFLUENCES/ EDUCATION

DOMESTIC AFFAIRS

QUESTIONING, THINKING & DECIDING

PLEASURE & ROMANCE

ONE-TO-ONE RELATIONSHIPS

EFFECTIVE WORK & HEALTH

JANUARY HIGHS AND LOWS

Here I show you how the rhythms of the Moon will affect you this month. Like the tide, your energies and abilities will rise and fall with its pattern. When it is above the centre line, go for it, when it is below, you should be resting.

HIGH 5TH–6TH

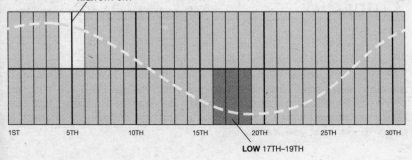

1ST   5TH   10TH   15TH   20TH   25TH   30TH

LOW 17TH–19TH

31 MONDAY
Moon Age Day 18 Moon Sign Leo

am...

pm...

Things should be looking good – so much so that you might not even bother with New Year's resolutions! For the moment you can afford to make life up as you go along. There are considerable gains to be made on a material level. It's a question of making the most of some good luck, together with your razor-sharp intuition.

1 TUESDAY
Moon Age Day 19 Moon Sign Leo

am...

pm...

Practical assistance could be hard to come by today, and if this proves to be the case your best resort is clearly to help yourself. This might mean riding roughshod over the opinions of specific individuals, not a practice in which you would indulge as a rule. As long as you know you are justified, some action may be necessary.

2 WEDNESDAY
Moon Age Day 20 Moon Sign Virgo

am...

pm...

While professional matters now seem to have less going for them, the days in view might appear to hold a great deal more scope for an enjoyable social life. Take advantage of any invitations that are offered, and be ready to grab them with both hands. Mixing with people you don't know very well is particularly well starred.

3 THURSDAY
Moon Age Day 21 Moon Sign Virgo

am...

pm...

The most rewarding periods now come through home matters, and through issues associated with personal relationships. You can't expect everyone to fall in automatically with your way of thinking, but you clearly are blessed with a silver tongue at this time and should be using it to try to get what you want.

4 FRIDAY
Moon Age Day 22 Moon Sign Virgo

am ....

pm...

It isn't out of the question that some Librans will now be thinking about taking a very early holiday. Any opportunity to get away from the cold and to go somewhere warm would be quite welcome. Even if the journey has to be in your mind for the time being, the excursion could prove to be interesting.

5 SATURDAY
Moon Age Day 23 Moon Sign Libra

am ....

pm...

It's time to push ahead with all your most important schemes. The lunar high is around, and that means general good luck is there for the taking. The spotlight is on looking and feeling great, and on your ability to take the social world by storm. You have what it takes to get through a great deal of work right now.

6 SUNDAY
Moon Age Day 24 Moon Sign Libra

am ....

pm...

Now you can afford to apply yourself, ahead of what has potential to be a very favourable week. If you are willing to stick up for people you know to be in the right, you might be surprised at the positive reactions that you can attract. Keep away from negative types and go for gold in any new venture.

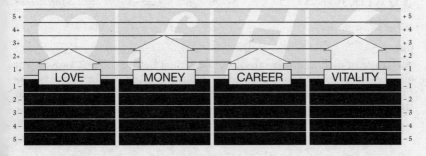

7 MONDAY
Moon Age Day 25 Moon Sign Scorpio

am ....

pm ....

In terms of career you could register a few setbacks now. These shouldn't last long or prove to be particularly serious, though they may necessitate you taking action you have avoided previously. Don't be tempted to get involved in actual rule breaking, though it might be necessary to just bend a few!

8 TUESDAY
Moon Age Day 26 Moon Sign Scorpio

am ....

pm ....

Are you giving the impression that you are only concerned with your own ideas right now? Perhaps you are, particularly if you know for sure that you have right on your side. Get ahead with any tasks you don't like, leaving yourself with more time later in the day to spend doing what you really want.

9 WEDNESDAY
Moon Age Day 27 Moon Sign Sagittarius

am ....

pm ....

This is a period during which you can focus squarely on yourself. Being selfish goes against the natural Libran grain, but with the Sun in your solar fourth house you should at least be willing to think about feathering your own nest. Keeping a sense of proportion isn't too easy for now, particularly when it comes to romance.

10 THURSDAY
Moon Age Day 28 Moon Sign Sagittarius

am ....

pm ....

A change of plan might be absolutely essential before today is out. Don't allow matters to get too staid, and be willing to listen to alternative points of view. There is an element of absentmindedness around at present, so there is much to be said for remembering to write things down.

11 FRIDAY
Moon Age Day 29 Moon Sign Capricorn

am ....

pm ....

Trends suggest you can be at your best in social and romantic situations now, and can gain tremendously from simply being in the right place at the right time. Keep your eyes and ears open and be willing to take whatever chance is necessary in order to get yourself into the good books of important or influential people.

12 SATURDAY
Moon Age Day 0 Moon Sign Capricorn

am ....

pm ....

Though some spendthrift tendencies are possible, in a general sense you should be able to strengthen your finances now. Maybe as a result of action you took in the past, or possibly through simple good luck, you have a chance to improve your financial situation. Even if you can't make progress now, it is important to keep your eyes open.

13 SUNDAY
Moon Age Day 1 Moon Sign Aquarius

am ....

pm ....

You are prepared to work very hard for what you want right now. Because your mind works in several different directions at the same time, ensure that you are looking at all possible eventualities. Don't be in the least surprised if you find your general popularity to be extremely high at present.

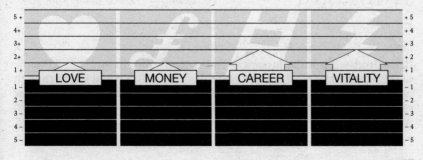

14 MONDAY
Moon Age Day 2 Moon Sign Aquarius

am...

pm...

Socially speaking you now embark upon a busier period. You should be less inclined to retreat into your shell and have what it takes to hold your own in any company. You can thank the position of Mars for these trends. Make the week work for you by taking social and romantic opportunities the moment they arise.

15 TUESDAY
Moon Age Day 3 Moon Sign Pisces

am...

pm...

Small speculations can be made to work on your behalf. That doesn't necessarily mean you have to spend too much time thinking about gambling. On the contrary, the accent is on simply having a good time. Romance is well accented, as is your ability to come to terms with people from all walks of life. Enjoy what the day offers.

16 WEDNESDAY
Moon Age Day 4 Moon Sign Pisces

am...

pm...

In some ways, you are probably rather ahead of yourself at the moment, so you can afford to take stock of situations more than would generally be the case. It's all very well having big plans in your mind, but it is going to take some time to get them off the ground. Today would be ideal for seeking support.

17 THURSDAY
Moon Age Day 5 Moon Sign Aries

am...

pm...

Before today is out the lunar low comes along and that might take some of the wind out of your sails for a couple of days. You could feel as though events are not going your way, though you need to consider the part your own attitude is playing in the situation. Popularity is within your grasp in relationships now.

18 FRIDAY
Moon Age Day 6 Moon Sign Aries

am ....

pm..

Even if you're still not moving any mountains, it pays to be on the look-out for some interesting and potentially lucrative news, which could come along at any time now. Remember that your recent hard work should enable you to reap the rewards you have been seeking before very long, and you need to be ready.

19 SATURDAY
Moon Age Day 7 Moon Sign Aries

am ....

pm..

Creative potential counts for a great deal now, as does your sense of order and harmony. In relationships, taking up your usual position as peacemaker can make all the difference, and you should be making a good impression on just about anyone. Don't be fooled by promises of gains without effort. They're probably groundless.

20 SUNDAY
Moon Age Day 8 Moon Sign Taurus

am ....

pm..

Domestically speaking there could well be plenty going on, and since the lunar low is now out of the way the path towards a greater sense of enjoyment is clear. Confidence is emphasised, and although it is still early in the year, it isn't beyond reason that you would welcome some time out of doors.

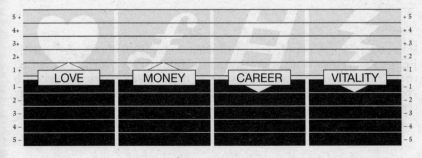

21 MONDAY
Moon Age Day 9 Moon Sign Taurus

am ....

pm ....

Routines are probably out of the window today, as you are encouraged to opt for a new and different period. You need change and diversity, and can push the added zing that is on offer at present in a number of different directions. Showing others how good you are to have around should come naturally to you now.

22 TUESDAY
Moon Age Day 10 Moon Sign Gemini

am ....

pm ....

Creatively speaking you can be on top form today, and might decide the time is right to make some changes in and around your home. If decorating is on the cards, an imaginative approach is definitely the order of the day. Whether everyone in the family agrees remains to be seen, and some persuasion may be required.

23 WEDNESDAY
Moon Age Day 11 Moon Sign Gemini

am ....

pm ....

Today is fairly neutral, allowing you scope to find your own way through the day in whatever manner you think best. If you want others on board, you might have to gee them on. Try to stay away from everyday routines, some of which could prove extremely tedious right now.

24 THURSDAY
Moon Age Day 12 Moon Sign Gemini

am ....

pm ....

Getting to know people is part of what today is all about, particularly in a social sense. With stimulation available at every turn, it might be hard to concentrate on the matter at hand. Maybe you should curb your excitement, just in case not everything turns out quite the way you had expected.

25 FRIDAY   *Moon Age Day 13 Moon Sign Cancer*

am ....

pm ....

Volunteering is all very well, though you need to bear in mind that others will take you at your word and you might end up far busier than you expected. Even if you are your usual, cheery self, you may not feel quite as 'in tune' with life as usual today. Everyone needs a rest now and again, and today could be your time.

26 SATURDAY   *Moon Age Day 14 Moon Sign Cancer*

am ....

pm ....

There are good reasons to focus on romance this weekend. If you are a young or young-at-heart Libran, with no attachments, this is the time to keep your eyes open. The more settled among you could almost certainly reap new rewards from existing ties. Be willing to listen to what family members have to say.

27 SUNDAY   *Moon Age Day 15 Moon Sign Leo*

am ....

pm ....

There are some strategic gains to be made today, particularly in relationships. It's in your interests to ensure that others don't misconstrue what you are trying to say, so it's worth trying hard to get your message across intact. In true Libran style, your attitude should be balanced and very fair.

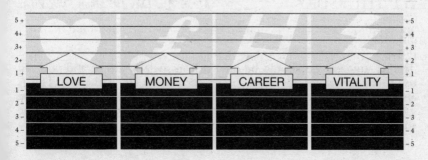

28 MONDAY
Moon Age Day 16   Moon Sign Leo

am..

pm..

With a new working week in view, you should be starting as you mean to go on, though until tomorrow, energy could be in short supply. In any sphere of life, you would be better off using today to plan, so that tomorrow, under better planetary trends, you can really put your ideas to the test.

29 TUESDAY
Moon Age Day 17   Moon Sign Virgo

am..

pm..

People who are important to you should figure prominently in your thinking today. It's time to use the energy you have available and to show your determination to get ahead. Confronting issues that have a bearing on your family life is fine, though it pays to consult those concerned before taking any action.

30 WEDNESDAY
Moon Age Day 18   Moon Sign Virgo

am..

pm..

Routines might be something of a bind today. This relates to a desire on your part to be free to pursue whatever interests are uppermost in your mind at present. This could make it difficult to concentrate on irrelevant details. Patience is required, and let's face it – you have more of that than most people!

31 THURSDAY
Moon Age Day 19   Moon Sign Virgo

am..

pm..

Trends suggest you should be on a roll in social matters, and you can use today to bring your usual sparkle to bear on any gathering. This is also an ideal time to co-operate in work ventures, some of which can be given an added boost, perhaps as a result of the intervention of some surprising people.

1 FRIDAY
Moon Age Day 20 Moon Sign Libra

am..

pm..

This has potential to be the most positive time of the month. The lunar high allows you to make use of that excellent personality, not only in a professional sense, but personally too. It wouldn't be fair to suggest that you will get everything your heart desires, but you certainly have scope to achieve some little triumphs.

2 SATURDAY
Moon Age Day 21 Moon Sign Libra

am..

pm..

Enthusiasm reaches an all-time high and you have what it takes to get ahead in a big way. Rather than committing yourself to mundane tasks, be willing to go out and get what you really want from life. Acting on impulse is something you are generally quite good at, but the ability is much enhanced today.

3 SUNDAY
Moon Age Day 22 Moon Sign Scorpio

am..

pm..

Be ready to respond to any resistance to your views that you encounter today. It might help to treat this as a sort of test and keep in mind that if you lose your temper, then clearly you have failed. Strive to achieve a state of affairs in which you can use your Libran skill to talk others round to your own attitude.

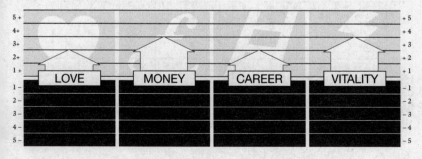

February
2013

Your Month at a Glance

(+) = Opportunities are around   ● = Be on the defensive   ● = Life is pretty ordinary

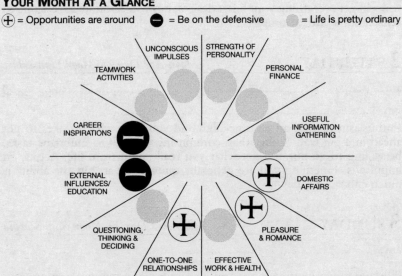

UNCONSCIOUS IMPULSES

STRENGTH OF PERSONALITY

TEAMWORK ACTIVITIES

PERSONAL FINANCE

CAREER INSPIRATIONS

USEFUL INFORMATION GATHERING

EXTERNAL INFLUENCES/ EDUCATION

DOMESTIC AFFAIRS

QUESTIONING, THINKING & DECIDING

PLEASURE & ROMANCE

ONE-TO-ONE RELATIONSHIPS

EFFECTIVE WORK & HEALTH

February Highs and Lows

Here I show you how the rhythms of the Moon will affect you this month. Like the tide, your energies and abilities will rise and fall with its pattern. When it is above the centre line, go for it, when it is below, you should be resting.

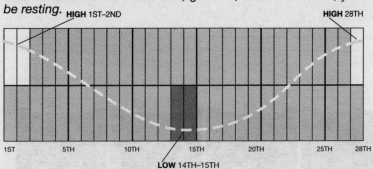

HIGH 1ST–2ND

HIGH 28TH

1ST   5TH   10TH   15TH   20TH   25TH   28TH

LOW 14TH–15TH

4 MONDAY *Moon Age Day 23 Moon Sign Scorpio*

am...

pm...

There could be a somewhat nostalgic phase coming your way. This is not especially unusual for Libra, and needn't really get in the way of living your life. The only drawback is that it could encourage a belief that there was once a wonderful world in which everything worked out right. In your heart you know this isn't the case.

5 TUESDAY *Moon Age Day 24 Moon Sign Sagittarius*

am...

pm...

Although in some ways your home life could be slightly less well ordered than you would wish, this is a short-term trend and so needn't have too much bearing on your day as a whole. Maybe you could save yourself some aggravation by choosing to mix with friends rather than relatives.

6 WEDNESDAY *Moon Age Day 25 Moon Sign Sagittarius*

am...

pm...

There is much to be said for striving to make this a more light-hearted day than yesterday. The emphasis seems to be on having fun and also allowing others to enjoy themselves. You might get on especially well with younger people, or the type of individual who has an unorthodox way of behaving.

7 THURSDAY *Moon Age Day 26 Moon Sign Capricorn*

am...

pm...

Today is a chance to allow intimate and private matters to take centre stage. That might mean you have to withdraw somewhat from the more sociable qualities that have predominated of late. Everyone needs to slow down sometime, and this is just as true for Libra as for any other zodiac sign.

8 FRIDAY

Moon Age Day 27 Moon Sign Capricorn

am..

pm..

It may pay to try to broaden your horizons in some way now. Do whatever you can to open yourself up to the wider world and don't turn away any reasonable offer of advancement. So many people have no idea what they can do until they put themselves to the test – and this is typical of the mind-set of many Librans.

9 SATURDAY

Moon Age Day 28 Moon Sign Aquarius

am..

pm..

The domestic sphere of your life now begins to offer benefits once again. This would also be an excellent time for mixing business with pleasure. Part of your appeal right now is your ability to get along well with most people, though that's not to say this will extend to those who are particularly arrogant.

10 SUNDAY

Moon Age Day 0 Moon Sign Aquarius

am..

pm..

Pleasure pursuits and romance are well marked now. It's up to you to make the most of them, and to consider leaving certain other matters to one side for the time being. The Air-sign quality of friendliness is highlighted, and getting on well with others should once again be a natural aspect of life.

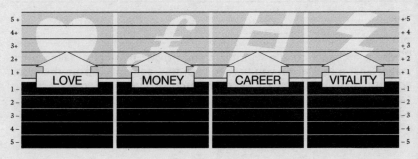

11 MONDAY *Moon Age Day 1 Moon Sign Pisces*

am..

pm..

Don't be surprised if your work routines are disrupted by some unexpected mishaps. Even if none of these are anything more than temporary hiccups, you will still need to deal with them. Your best approach is to retain that famous Libran sense of humour. Being able to laugh at yourself is vitally important.

12 TUESDAY *Moon Age Day 2 Moon Sign Pisces*

am..

pm..

Once again it might be difficult for you to avoid the odd mishap where practical matters are concerned. Focusing on romantic opportunities can certainly help you to counter these less than favourable trends. Your popularity remains generally high, and it is possible to impress someone who has been quite important to you recently.

13 WEDNESDAY *Moon Age Day 3 Moon Sign Pisces*

am..

pm..

There is room today to show how enterprising – and funny – you can be, though you need to beware any tendency towards absentmindedness. The lunar low is just around the corner, so energy could be slightly lacking at this stage of the working week. For this reason alone, focusing on jobs at home might be your best option.

14 THURSDAY *Moon Age Day 4 Moon Sign Aries*

am..

pm..

Important decisions will probably have to wait. The lunar low does nothing to help you make progress, either today or tomorrow. As a result you may as well decide to slow down and watch life go by for a while. Meanwhile, make the most of the assistance you can obtain from colleagues and friends.

15 FRIDAY
Moon Age Day 5 Moon Sign Aries

am ....

pm ....

The lunar low continues, and that encourages you to settle for a quieter interlude. This time around you shouldn't feel too curtailed by this trend, particularly if you feel ready for a break. An ideal day to watch life go by, while you stand on the sidelines and plan your moves for later. Be willing to seek support from family members.

16 SATURDAY
Moon Age Day 6 Moon Sign Taurus

am ....

pm ....

You can afford to put yourself in the limelight today, and it's time for Libra to show what it is really worth, especially in social and professional situations. There is much to be said for allowing deeper attachments to take something of a back seat, particularly if those who are normally closest to you seem rather distant for now.

17 SUNDAY
Moon Age Day 7 Moon Sign Taurus

am ....

pm ....

Don't be shy today. Bear in mind that people may be watching you, and it is important for you to shine. This is especially true in a work sense, but you can't rule out the possibility that you will attract some romantic admirers too. There are small gains to be made financially, but you will have to keep your eyes open.

18 MONDAY
Moon Age Day 8 Moon Sign Gemini

am ....

pm ....

Trends suggest that you may not take kindly to being told what to do now. However, it pays to remain fairly tolerant, and not to blame the messenger when new instructions come along. Remember that others are only following the orders they have been given. It isn't like Libra to be resentful, though it can't be ruled out today.

19 TUESDAY
Moon Age Day 9 Moon Sign Gemini

am ....

pm ....

There's nothing wrong with being slightly more liberal with money now, particularly if it's for a good cause. A quieter approach works well today, though that needn't stop you from recognising a bargain and snapping it up. For this reason alone, there is much to be said for a spot of shopping!

20 WEDNESDAY
Moon Age Day 10 Moon Sign Gemini

am ....

pm ....

Don't be too quick to jump to conclusions right now. It's all very well believing you have all the answers, but it might be difficult to find the degree of good fortune you need to back up your hunches. As a result, it would be sensible to seek sound advice and to give matters a degree of careful thought.

21 THURSDAY
Moon Age Day 11 Moon Sign Cancer

am ....

pm ....

Anything old or unusual seems to have a particular fascination for you today. Your inventiveness is also well accented, assisting you to come up with innovative ideas that you can follow up later. Be willing to share some of your schemes with people who are more in the know than you are – you may learn something.

22 FRIDAY
Moon Age Day 12 Moon Sign Cancer

am ....

pm ....

A new trend can have a bearing on your general attitude towards life as a whole, as the Sun enters your solar sixth house. This emphasises your practical abilities, and might even allow you extra input when it comes to moving the goalposts. If you have made up your mind about something, don't take no for an answer.

23 SATURDAY ☿
Moon Age Day 13 Moon Sign Leo

am ....

pm ....

The weekend brings a burst of enthusiasm for subject matter that hasn't played any particular part in your life up to now. Ringing the changes is very important for Libra, and especially so at the moment. Care and attention to detail in any sphere of your life is likely to pay handsome dividends later.

24 SUNDAY ☿
Moon Age Day 14 Moon Sign Leo

am ....

pm ....

If your boredom threshold is still low, it's up to you to look for entertaining possibilities and not tie yourself down with too many routine and tedious tasks. Your ability to talk the hind leg off a donkey can assist you to make more friends, particularly if you make sure you always have something interesting to say!

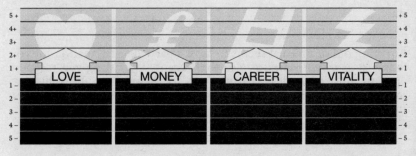

25 MONDAY ☿ *Moon Age Day 15 Moon Sign Leo*

am..

pm..

Routines are necessary today, though not necessarily enjoyable. You can now afford to ring the changes and to opt for a different way of looking at matters. It's worth giving yourself a pat on the back for recent successes, though beware of allowing anything to go to your head. Keep pushing forward.

26 TUESDAY ☿ *Moon Age Day 16 Moon Sign Virgo*

am..

pm..

It's time to stand up for yourself, especially if you feel you are up against people who have a bullying attitude to life. You needn't allow others to push you around, and can afford to do what's necessary to protect those you see as being more vulnerable than yourself. Before you speak, make sure you are in full possession of facts.

27 WEDNESDAY ☿ *Moon Age Day 17 Moon Sign Virgo*

am..

pm..

Home and family means a good deal to Libra, and even more than usual now. It's natural to worry somewhat about particular family members, but remember that things often turn out better than you expected. Financial good luck may be hard to find at the moment, so it pays to guard your resources carefully.

28 THURSDAY ☿ *Moon Age Day 18 Moon Sign Libra*

am..

pm..

Now would seem to be a particularly good time to put your luck to the test. The lunar high supports you, or at any rate assists you to find the confidence to take that extra chance. Social trends look excellent, as do the prospects for love in your life. If routines don't hold any appeal, be prepared to shelve them for today.

1 FRIDAY ☿ *Moon Age Day 19 Moon Sign Libra*

am ....

pm ....

The first day of March offers you a good start to the month and has potential to be an enormously enjoyable period from a personal point of view. If you have an opportunity to put yourself in the public eye, do what you can to give a good account of yourself. This is rarely difficult for friendly, communicative Libra.

2 SATURDAY ☿ *Moon Age Day 20 Moon Sign Scorpio*

am ....

pm ....

It's time to get down to brass tacks, even if there are some people who aren't keen on you doing so. A period of reorganisation is at hand, and you can't expect everyone to respond positively to this. However, once you have decided on a specific course of action, you needn't allow anything to change your mind.

3 SUNDAY ☿ *Moon Age Day 21 Moon Sign Scorpio*

am ....

pm ....

You could find intimate relationships far more rewarding today than casual friendships. There are some people on whom you are quite willing to rely, and though the suspicious side of your nature is to the fore at present, it is to these individuals that you should turn. Financially speaking, better fortune is within your grasp.

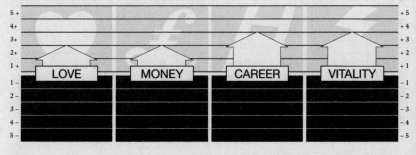

March

2013

YOUR MONTH AT A GLANCE

$\oplus$ = Opportunities are around $\ominus$ = Be on the defensive   ◯ = Life is pretty ordinary

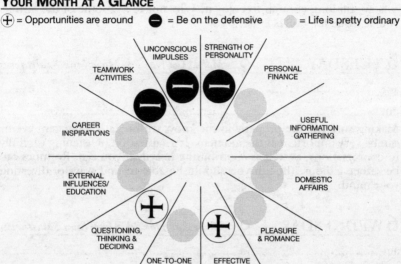

MARCH HIGHS AND LOWS

Here I show you how the rhythms of the Moon will affect you this month. Like the tide, your energies and abilities will rise and fall with its pattern. When it is above the centre line, go for it, when it is below, you should be resting.

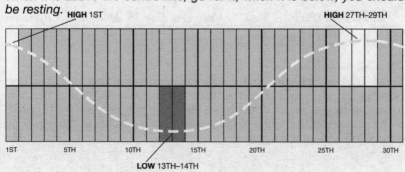

4 MONDAY ☿   *Moon Age Day 22 Moon Sign Sagittarius*

am ....

pm ....

Once again, trends suggest that your most rewarding moments could come via love and romance. This can be a very stimulating sort of day in a number of respects. A desire for luxury is indicated, plus a willingness to stay still long enough to enjoy it! Why not call in some of the favours you've done for others in the past?

5 TUESDAY ☿   *Moon Age Day 23 Moon Sign Sagittarius*

am ....

pm ....

Making sure you are properly in the know with regard to current events can be very important at the moment. It's a question of listening carefully to conversations, as well as contributing heavily if you can. Routines can be rather tedious, though you should be able to find ways of diverting your mind.

6 WEDNESDAY ☿   *Moon Age Day 24 Moon Sign Sagittarius*

am ....

pm ....

You really do have to make room for the emotions of others. Generally that's not a tall order for Libra, but present planetary trends encourage a slightly more selfish approach than would usually be the case. Look for opportunities to strengthen your finances at present.

7 THURSDAY ☿   *Moon Age Day 25 Moon Sign Capricorn*

am ....

pm ....

Today it is co-operative and collaborative ventures that offer the best possibilities. The year is growing older and you may decide that the time has come to get out of doors more. Sporting ventures are well starred, with the competitive edge of Libra now firmly on display, and showing particularly well in team games.

YOUR DAILY GUIDE TO MARCH 2013

8 FRIDAY ☿ *Moon Age Day 26 Moon Sign Capricorn*

am..

pm..

Bear in mind that strong words can turn into domestic discussions or even arguments if you are not careful. There's a fine line between being touchy and sticking up for what you know is right. Some care is necessary, because your opinions today could so easily change even before tomorrow comes along.

9 SATURDAY ☿ *Moon Age Day 27 Moon Sign Aquarius*

am..

pm..

A good period for useful information gathering. This can come from the common interaction you have with the world at large, or perhaps even through a tendency to be nosy at present. If there is something you want especially, find someone who can help you and summon up the courage to ask.

10 SUNDAY ☿ *Moon Age Day 28 Moon Sign Aquarius*

am..

pm..

In contrast to previous trends, you may now take comfort from whatever is going on in your home life that is reassuring, familiar and secure. This may not be an exciting interlude but it has potential to be quite rewarding in its own way. The support of loved ones can, in itself, feel like a protecting arm around your shoulder.

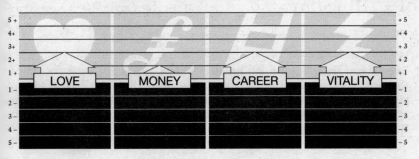

63

11 MONDAY ☿ *Moon Age Day 29 Moon Sign Pisces*

am..

pm..

Expect to make the most of a particularly upbeat phase. Today offers the best of both worlds because you should be getting on well, both at home and at work. Keeping ahead of the game is important, especially where sporting or professional activities are concerned. Try not to be anxious about unnecessary details.

12 TUESDAY ☿ *Moon Age Day 0 Moon Sign Pisces*

am..

pm..

It's worth making sure you accomplish as much as you can early in the day. This part of the week works best as a social time, and you should also have a chance to achieve your full potential personally speaking. Romance is distinctly possible, and there are friends around who would probably love the chance to be of use to you.

13 WEDNESDAY ☿ *Moon Age Day 1 Moon Sign Aries*

am..

pm..

Today could well mark a low point in your fortunes. This is entirely due to the position of the Moon and is best dealt with by curtailing your spending. You can't expect to achieve everything that you want right now, but if you keep up a good level of friendly co-operation, you might not actually realise this fact.

14 THURSDAY ☿ *Moon Age Day 2 Moon Sign Aries*

am..

pm..

Even if you are still not firing on all cylinders, this is not a state of affairs that will prevent you from getting on well in all areas of your life. If you decide to concentrate on friendship, and perhaps also on closer attachments still, there are good times to be had. Speculation of any sort is probably not wise.

15 FRIDAY ☿ *Moon Age Day 3 Moon Sign Taurus*

am..

pm..

You may feel you need some sort of division between personal obligations and the demands that the outside world is making on you at this time. Try to achieve that sensible balance for which your zodiac sign is justifiably famous. At the same time it is clear that you need distinct periods of meditation.

16 SATURDAY ☿ *Moon Age Day 4 Moon Sign Taurus*

am..

pm..

Beware of allowing your home to become a battleground. It would be better to stay away from possible situations of confrontation, at least for now. Even spending time on your own is better than falling out with others. There is much to be said for finding something better to do with your weekend!

17 SUNDAY ☿ *Moon Age Day 5 Moon Sign Taurus*

am..

pm..

Focusing on matters that are close to your heart would be no bad thing this weekend, though you needn't allow this to get in the way of your desire to have a good time. You can afford to leave aside some of the less important routines that could tend to cloud the day, and be prepared to move at a moment's notice.

	LOVE	MONEY	CAREER	VITALITY
5 +				+ 5
4+				+ 4
3+				+ 3
2+				+ 2
1 +				+ 1
1 –				– 1
2 –				– 2
3 –				– 3
4 –				– 4
5 –				– 5

18 MONDAY ☿ *Moon Age Day 6 Moon Sign Gemini*

am ....

pm ....

In professional matters especially, trends encourage you to avoid hasty actions and to think carefully before you make any move. Personally speaking, life should be somewhat easier and offers you the chance to make an important conquest. Single Librans especially can set out to make sure this is an eventful day.

19 TUESDAY *Moon Age Day 7 Moon Sign Gemini*

am ....

pm ....

It pays to keep a look-out for people you haven't seen for a while, as bringing them back into your life now could be quite fortuitous. Confronting issues from the past is a must at the moment because you are now in a position to straighten them out in your mind. It's time to dispel some of the things you have been worrying about.

20 WEDNESDAY *Moon Age Day 8 Moon Sign Cancer*

am ....

pm ....

Be prepared to put things right that you know should have been done and finished previously. In some instances this isn't your fault, and you may be inclined to feel resentful about this. Don't waste time dwelling on the fact that you are correcting mistakes made by other people, simply get on with it. It isn't fair – but that's life!

21 THURSDAY *Moon Age Day 9 Moon Sign Cancer*

am ....

pm ....

The Sun enters your solar seventh house today. This is purely and simply an ideal time to make relationships work better. For the next month or so it is generally easy to get onside with others and to offer them a better insight into the way you function. Stand by for the chance to create another romantic interlude today.

22 FRIDAY
Moon Age Day 10   Moon Sign Cancer

am ....

pm..

You have scope to come up with plenty of ingenious ideas today. Although there may not be too much you can do about them at the moment, you should have your thinking head on today and could easily spend some time planning. New hobbies or interests that surface again in your life are highlighted now.

23 SATURDAY
Moon Age Day 11   Moon Sign Leo

am ....

pm..

Joint finances are one area of life that you are encouraged to address today. This may not interest you very much, but such things have to be done. It's a question of balance, though. You can sugar the pill by giving yourself one very enjoyable task for every one that doesn't please you so much.

24 SUNDAY
Moon Age Day 12   Moon Sign Leo

am ....

pm..

A continuing trend of potentially improved finances is partly due to planetary influence but also responds to a very responsible attitude on your part. Why not continue this process by dealing with family monetary issues? You can't expect everyone to be pleased with what you have to say, but it's important to carry on anyway.

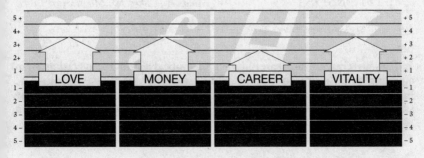

25 MONDAY
Moon Age Day 13 Moon Sign Virgo

am...

pm...

Family life is well accented today and you are in a position to sort out any little problems at home that have been building up for a few days. There are good reasons to find time to get to know younger family members better, as they grow up so quickly. Friends should be welcome, but they might have to come to you.

26 TUESDAY
Moon Age Day 14 Moon Sign Virgo

am...

pm...

Your ability to get onside with others is emphasised, and you need to make the most of it. Personality issues are to the fore. It's sometimes difficult to discover whether you are making the sort of impression that really counts, though before today is out you should be in no doubt about what you have achieved.

27 WEDNESDAY
Moon Age Day 15 Moon Sign Libra

am...

pm...

Information you can gather from friends simply has to be listened to now. It's natural to have a few doubts about the integrity of certain individuals, but that doesn't necessarily mean they are always going to let you down. It's all a matter of trust, and that's something you should be prepared to demonstrate now.

28 THURSDAY
Moon Age Day 16 Moon Sign Libra

am...

pm...

It pays to concentrate carefully on the job at hand today rather than allowing your mind to wander. This situation doesn't last long. The lunar high continues to offer you the chance to go for gold in almost any situation. It's all a question of using the luck that is available and being ready to chance your arm where appropriate.

29 FRIDAY
Moon Age Day 17 Moon Sign Libra

am ....

pm...

You have what it takes to get important undertakings to go as planned. The lunar high supports your efforts in a number of directions and assists you to tap into a higher degree of luck. Actually you are making most of your own luck as you go along. Don't cause problems for yourself with a slight tendency to rush things rather too much.

30 SATURDAY
Moon Age Day 18 Moon Sign Scorpio

am ....

pm...

The start of the weekend can be zippy and interesting. Mixing with those individuals who have a similar attitude to life is well starred, but that doesn't mean you can't get to know newcomers. Concentrate on the matter at hand in business, but don't rule out the opportunity to take advantage of good social trends later.

31 SUNDAY
Moon Age Day 19 Moon Sign Scorpio

am ....

pm...

Today works best if you avoid taking anyone or anything particularly seriously. You have plenty of get-up-and-go, but that might not be enough on its own to make the sort of general progress you seek. All the same, when it comes to the popularity stakes, you need to make sure you are tops with as many people as possible.

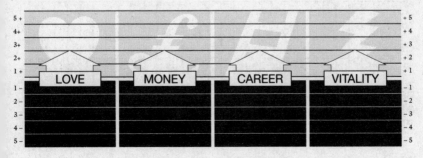

April

2013

YOUR MONTH AT A GLANCE

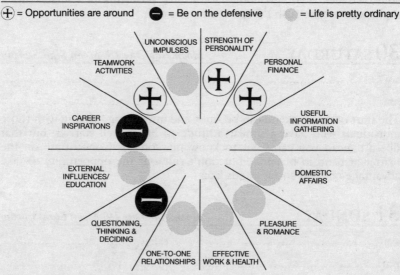

⊕ = Opportunities are around   ⊖ = Be on the defensive   ⬤ = Life is pretty ordinary

UNCONSCIOUS IMPULSES
STRENGTH OF PERSONALITY
TEAMWORK ACTIVITIES
PERSONAL FINANCE
CAREER INSPIRATIONS
USEFUL INFORMATION GATHERING
EXTERNAL INFLUENCES/ EDUCATION
DOMESTIC AFFAIRS
QUESTIONING, THINKING & DECIDING
PLEASURE & ROMANCE
ONE-TO-ONE RELATIONSHIPS
EFFECTIVE WORK & HEALTH

APRIL HIGHS AND LOWS

Here I show you how the rhythms of the Moon will affect you this month. Like the tide, your energies and abilities will rise and fall with its pattern. When it is above the centre line, go for it, when it is below, you should be resting.

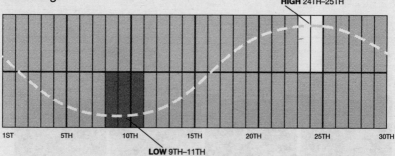

HIGH 24TH–25TH

LOW 9TH–11TH

1ST   5TH   10TH   15TH   20TH   25TH   30TH

1 MONDAY
Moon Age Day 20 Moon Sign Sagittarius

am ....

pm..

You are entering a much brisker period now and one in which you can free yourself from any minor setbacks you have registered recently. Don't take too much notice of the odd individual who thinks you are doing things wrongly. The proof of the pudding is in the eating, so be prepared to demonstrate that your way is correct.

2 TUESDAY
Moon Age Day 21 Moon Sign Sagittarius

am ....

pm..

The impulse for personal freedom is now extremely strong. It might be very difficult to resist simply dropping everything and taking a trip. This restless side to your character is something that is highlighted on a number of occasions at the moment. Things can be helped by simply breaking usual routines.

3 WEDNESDAY
Moon Age Day 22 Moon Sign Capricorn

am ....

pm..

Keep your opinions to yourself, especially if you are in company that doesn't always agree with your zany side, which is definitely to the fore at present. You can buy yourself some more time later by putting in that extra bit of effort right now. Several jobs at once should be a piece of cake!

4 THURSDAY
Moon Age Day 23 Moon Sign Capricorn

am ....

pm..

Partnerships could turn out to be especially lucky at the moment. This may relate to personal attachments, but is just as likely to be relevant to work-based affiliations. Today works best if you set out to have a good time and talk as much as you can. Getting people to listen is another matter, but one that should be within your abilities at the moment.

5 FRIDAY
Moon Age Day 24 Moon Sign Aquarius

am..

pm..

Work and practical matters can now be moved on smoothly, and it shouldn't be hard to find the sort of support you really need. Look for excitement in almost any form and if you get the chance, be willing to take a journey. Plan now for the weekend and make certain that your intentions include having fun.

6 SATURDAY
Moon Age Day 25 Moon Sign Aquarius

am..

pm..

Personal relationships should still be on a roll, and you can use this trend to help you to get along well with just about anyone you encounter. It's time to display the very warm side of your nature, and to show that you are willing on this Saturday to listen to what people are saying. Popularity is the name of the game.

7 SUNDAY
Moon Age Day 26 Moon Sign Pisces

am..

pm..

The current emphasis being on your social life, it might be tempting to spend rather more money than you may have intended. If so, your best approach is to cast around. There are many interesting things you can find to do that will cost you nothing at all. Ask your friends too, because they may have some good ideas.

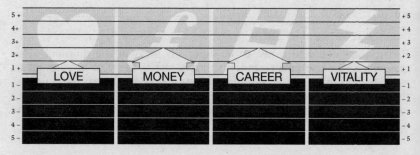

8 MONDAY
Moon Age Day 27 Moon Sign Pisces

am ....

pm...

You may find this to be a rather challenging day, but you can enjoy it all the same. You need to be in the sort of mood that allows you to push ahead progressively, and you shouldn't allow yourself to be deterred from taking any necessary course of action. At the same time, your pleasant nature can make all the difference.

9 TUESDAY
Moon Age Day 28 Moon Sign Aries

am ....

pm...

The lunar low encourages you to conserve your energies and leave all-important decisions for a few days. Sit back and watch life for a while, all the time thinking carefully and planning forward moves. Even if not everyone has your best interests at heart, you should know who you can turn to with genuine confidence.

10 WEDNESDAY
Moon Age Day 0 Moon Sign Aries

am ....

pm...

As the lunar low continues, be ready to deal with a few setbacks and some delays which might be impossible to counter. Try to stay cool, calm and collected, even if it feels as though too many demands are being made of you. You can help things along by choosing the company of people who have a positive outlook.

11 THURSDAY
Moon Age Day 1 Moon Sign Aries

am ....

pm...

By the middle of the today the horizon looks clearer and you should be pushing forward with a greater sense of certainty. There's a question of whether your nervous system will be quite as strong at the moment as it was earlier in the month. Don't be afraid to seek support from both loved ones and friends if required.

12 FRIDAY

Moon Age Day 2 Moon Sign Taurus

am ....

pm ....

The most rewarding periods today come through the intimacy you feel with others. Getting onside should be easier, even with people you've found difficult of late, and you may have an ability to shine in social situations. If others accuse you of taking a somewhat ruthless approach, ask yourself whether they have their own axe to grind.

13 SATURDAY

Moon Age Day 3 Moon Sign Taurus

am ....

pm ....

Keeping an eye on work related matters might be slightly difficult at the weekend, particularly if you are determined to have a good time at present. Achieving the degree of relaxation you require might not be particularly easy, especially since there are likely to be other demands on your time.

14 SUNDAY

Moon Age Day 4 Moon Sign Gemini

am ....

pm ....

Professional situations could well have you on the run, and it will be up to you to put in that extra bit of effort if you want to succeed. There are some tasks that you would be well advised to leave to others, at least for the time being. There isn't much point in considering yourself to be master of everything.

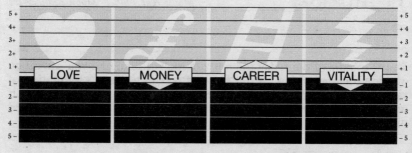

15 MONDAY

Moon Age Day 5 Moon Sign Gemini

am...

pm...

A variety of interests would do you good today, so avoid concentrating in only one direction. You are likely to be chatty, friendly and anxious to please. When you get the chance it might be an idea to get away from home, if only for an hour or two. The wide blue yonder begins to call you now.

16 TUESDAY

Moon Age Day 6 Moon Sign Gemini

am...

pm...

Creative pursuits should suit you down to the ground today. Maybe you are thinking about changes you want to make to your home, or just possibly contributing to a major refurbishment somewhere else, perhaps at work. Co-ordination is the order of the day, and this reflects in your taste.

17 WEDNESDAY

Moon Age Day 7 Moon Sign Cancer

am...

pm...

There should be a good deal of emphasis on the fun side of life now, and the middle of this working week offers opportunities for diversion. It pays to keep a sense of proportion if you have to deal with people who seem determined to be awkward. Remember that there is humour to be found in most situations.

18 THURSDAY

Moon Age Day 8 Moon Sign Cancer

am...

pm...

By all means make it plain to everyone that if things need sorting out, you are the person to do it. Just be careful, or you could bite off a good deal more than you can chew. The best way to approach any family arrangements that need to be made at the moment is through intensive and searching discussions.

19 FRIDAY

Moon Age Day 9 Moon Sign Leo

am..

pm..

Today offers scope to feel footloose and fancy-free, though of course if you are attached, you shouldn't necessarily extend this to your personal life. Nevertheless, the usual places and faces may not hold too much appeal for you. It's time for you to demonstrate the original qualities of your nature.

20 SATURDAY

Moon Age Day 10 Moon Sign Leo

am..

pm..

What matters the most at the moment is the opportunity to express yourself, and to ensure that the people you talk to understand your point of view only too well. You should be taking a very pragmatic view of life, and you may also remain quite convinced that you can tackle most jobs best if you do them yourself.

21 SUNDAY

Moon Age Day 11 Moon Sign Leo

am..

pm..

A day that lends itself to preparation and involves you looking carefully at all eventualities before you decide to move in any specific direction. Keep an eye open if you are going to the shops. There are bargains around at present, and it's simply a question of using your powers of observation to snap some of them up.

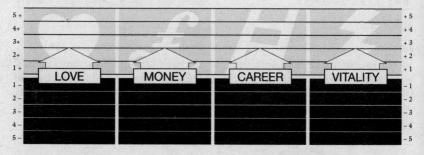

22 MONDAY   *Moon Age Day 12 Moon Sign Virgo*

am ....

pm...

This would be an ideal period for turning an interest into a lucrative sideline. Spend some time thinking about this, as you career through another busy day. Librans make the most of every minute, though they do also have a lazy streak. A diversion in the direction of luxury later in the day could appeal to you.

23 TUESDAY   *Moon Age Day 13 Moon Sign Virgo*

am ....

pm...

If you're ready for a change, and champing at the bit to get away from anything tedious or routine, you need to talk to family members and friends about getting away from it all in some way. An immediate change of scene would be ideal, but there is much to be said for travelling in your mind for the moment.

24 WEDNESDAY   *Moon Age Day 14 Moon Sign Libra*

am ....

pm...

Personal aims and ambitions on which you are focusing can more easily be addressed while the lunar high is about. You need to decide what you want from life, and to think about how you can get it. All you require is a little support, which should also be forthcoming, though remember that you have to ask for it.

25 THURSDAY   *Moon Age Day 15 Moon Sign Libra*

am ....

pm...

Good luck is there for the taking, courtesy of the lunar high. Make the most of favourable trends and push on towards what you really want from life. Keeping abreast of the way loved ones are thinking might be useful, and you can afford to let travel play a significant part in your thinking at this time.

26 FRIDAY
Moon Age Day 16 Moon Sign Scorpio

am...

pm...

It pays to avoid people who think they know everything. Getting along with such individuals might be difficult at the moment, given the certainty of your own mind and opinions. The combative side of your nature is emphasised at present, which could well be a puzzle to the people who know you well.

27 SATURDAY
Moon Age Day 17 Moon Sign Scorpio

am...

pm...

There's nothing wrong with a good argument, though you need to know when to call a halt, because there is a distinctly peace-loving quality to the Libran nature too. You have what it takes to deal with both necessities at present. There may be a prerequisite to stick with what you know for most of this weekend.

28 SUNDAY
Moon Age Day 18 Moon Sign Sagittarius

am...

pm...

This can be a very restless time, and one that doesn't particularly lend itself to relaxation. You need to redress the balance, maybe by way of strenuous exercise. Tiring out your body gives your mind the chance to slow down too. Look out for personalities who could have a bearing on your life at any time now.

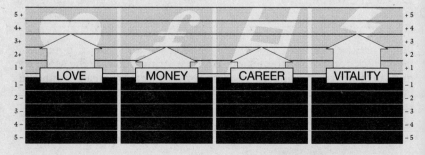

29 MONDAY   *Moon Age Day 19 Moon Sign Sagittarius*

am ....

pm...

If there is anything you can jettison from your life at the moment, the process could be more than worthwhile. You have a great deal going for you, but not if you are cluttered up with elements of the past that are of no further use. A spring clean is in order, and there is much to be said for starting on it now.

30 TUESDAY   *Moon Age Day 20 Moon Sign Capricorn*

am ....

pm...

Trends encourage you to focus on personal security at the moment. In addition, scepticism could be more evident than is usually the case for Libra. It might be best to make certain you don't get things out of proportion, because you work best when you remain trusting and open-minded.

1 WEDNESDAY   *Moon Age Day 21 Moon Sign Capricorn*

am ....

pm...

This is a time when relationships can prove to be very useful in a number of ways. There are gains to be made in terms of finances, perhaps by discussing plans with those closest to you, while new incentives at work assist you to make this part of the week very interesting and quite varied.

2 THURSDAY   *Moon Age Day 22 Moon Sign Aquarius*

am ....

pm...

Social matters are to the fore now, and it's a question of doing your best to join in the fun. You can't expect everyone to feel the same way, however, and you may have to deal with the odd grumpy type. Confidence remains high in a professional sense, and Librans looking for jobs should concentrate their efforts now.

3 FRIDAY
Moon Age Day 23 Moon Sign Aquarius

am ....

pm ....

Even if there are plenty of entertaining experiences on offer, it is possible that everything in the garden isn't quite so lovely in a home-based sense. You can't be expected to cater for everyone's wishes, and as long as you are doing your best, there isn't a great deal more that can be asked of you.

4 SATURDAY
Moon Age Day 24 Moon Sign Pisces

am ....

pm ....

The spotlight is now on your need to express yourself fully and quite dramatically. Because Libra is basically an easy-going type, any sudden outburst on your part is likely to shock. Maybe that's a good thing, because it lets people know that you are around and that you have good ideas of your own.

5 SUNDAY
Moon Age Day 25 Moon Sign Pisces

am ....

pm ....

Demanding obligations could force you to rethink some strategies, which comes hard at a time when you don't really want to concentrate on anything much at all. Your best approach is to keep things as simple as you can and enjoy a family-motivated weekend. A short trip to the coast or the country can work wonders.

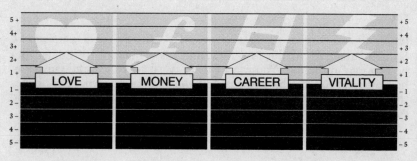

May

2013

YOUR MONTH AT A GLANCE

$\oplus$ = Opportunities are around $\ominus$ = Be on the defensive   = Life is pretty ordinary

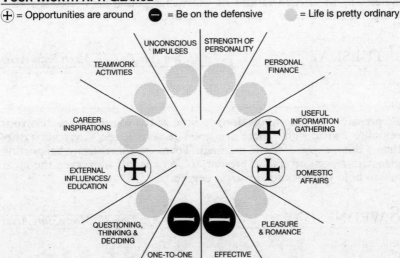

- UNCONSCIOUS IMPULSES
- STRENGTH OF PERSONALITY
- TEAMWORK ACTIVITIES
- PERSONAL FINANCE
- CAREER INSPIRATIONS
- USEFUL INFORMATION GATHERING $\oplus$
- EXTERNAL INFLUENCES/ EDUCATION $\oplus$
- DOMESTIC AFFAIRS $\oplus$
- QUESTIONING, THINKING & DECIDING
- ONE-TO-ONE RELATIONSHIPS $\ominus$
- EFFECTIVE WORK & HEALTH $\ominus$
- PLEASURE & ROMANCE

MAY HIGHS AND LOWS

Here I show you how the rhythms of the Moon will affect you this month. Like the tide, your energies and abilities will rise and fall with its pattern. When it is above the centre line, go for it, when it is below, you should be resting.

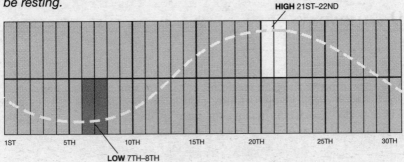

HIGH 21ST–22ND

LOW 7TH–8TH

1ST   5TH   10TH   15TH   20TH   25TH   30TH

6 MONDAY
Moon Age Day 26   Moon Sign Pisces

am...

pm...

Be careful when it comes to finding new solutions to old problems. It might be best in many ways to soldier on in your old way. Certainly innovation can be a good idea in some areas, though there are other spheres in which generations of experience count for more. It's all a matter of balance, and it's up to you to find it.

7 TUESDAY
Moon Age Day 27   Moon Sign Aries

am...

pm...

Be prepared to slow things down a little as the Moon moves into your opposite zodiac sign. There are good reasons to be a watcher rather than a doer, at least for the moment. There are some strong supporting planetary aspects around at present, so you needn't allow even the lunar low to hold you back to any great degree.

8 WEDNESDAY
Moon Age Day 28   Moon Sign Aries

am...

pm...

Spirits and vitality could still be in short supply. Go with the flow and don't allow yourself to be pushed into anything that goes against the grain. By late in the day tomorrow you can ensure that your energy is returning. In the meantime, your best approach is to spend your time quietly planning and looking ahead.

9 THURSDAY
Moon Age Day 29   Moon Sign Taurus

am...

pm...

This should prove to be an ideal time for capitalising on recent gains, and you have an excellent opportunity to firm up specific areas of your life. There is also a focus on making the most of the chance to increase your popularity. Make sure that you are the life and soul of most parties!

10 FRIDAY
Moon Age Day 0 Moon Sign Taurus

am...

pm...

By all means keep your options open in a general sense, though it pays to be firm in specific areas. Perhaps it's the case that other people are not living up to your expectations of them. As long as you know in your heart that you are being fair, there is nothing wrong with giving them a gentle prod.

11 SATURDAY
Moon Age Day 1 Moon Sign Gemini

am...

pm...

Emotional involvements could prove to be extremely satisfying at this time. The closer you are to a particular individual, the greater is your ability to ensure that things are working out well between you. Confidence should be available when you need it in a practical sense, and creative potential is also favoured.

12 SUNDAY
Moon Age Day 2 Moon Sign Gemini

am...

pm...

Trends assist you to achieve certain bonuses around this time. True, they might not be monetary in nature, but you ought to be able to enjoy them all the same. An ideal day for creating a good atmosphere at home and maybe even arranging a party. By tomorrow you may not be quite as energetic, so make the most of these trends.

13 MONDAY
Moon Age Day 3 Moon Sign Gemini

am ....

pm ....

You may still have to pace yourself a good deal as far as work is concerned. However, by the time the afternoon arrives you should be able to get back to your old self again. Get in gear and do something! It's time to try an exciting departure that you have shied away from in the past, and to marvel at your own courage.

14 TUESDAY
Moon Age Day 4 Moon Sign Cancer

am ....

pm ....

Any exchange of opinions could well prove to be extremely lively under present influences. That doesn't mean you have to be argumentative, though you can certainly afford to stick up for what you believe in. Are rules and regulations getting on your nerves? That's unusual for easy-going, law-abiding Libra.

15 WEDNESDAY
Moon Age Day 5 Moon Sign Cancer

am ....

pm ....

Solving certain problems has never been easier. You have the ability to use your mind like Sherlock Holmes at present, and should not dismiss your most intense feelings about anything. Analytical and yet at the same time sensitive to nuances, it's time to use these qualities to get inside the skin of those around you.

16 THURSDAY
Moon Age Day 6 Moon Sign Leo

am ....

pm ....

Personal confidence and flair shouldn't be lacking. All that might be missing at present is that final belief in yourself that is so important when you are viewed from the perspective of others. Why not use this evening to catch up with any outstanding tasks? It could leave you with more time to do what you want by the weekend.

17 FRIDAY
Moon Age Day 7 Moon Sign Leo

am ....

pm ....

You ought to be able to create a generally happy atmosphere around you now. It is possible for you to have the best of both worlds – success at work and contentment when in your own domain. Although you may feel yourself to be a thousand miles from a specific desire, perhaps it's really only just around the corner.

18 SATURDAY
Moon Age Day 8 Moon Sign Leo

am ....

pm ....

Today has much going for it. Make the most of a potentially busy weekend that offers the chance to tackle issues you might have found difficult to address earlier in the week. Go out and get what you want, especially in terms of relationships. Beware of exaggerating your sense of responsibility to family members now.

19 SUNDAY
Moon Age Day 9 Moon Sign Virgo

am ....

pm ....

If you have the chance to travel now, you should certainly consider doing so. A change of scene would suit your present mood wonderfully, the more so if you can put yourself in the company of people you like a great deal and who you find stimulating. What you don't need today is to be stuck in the same old rut.

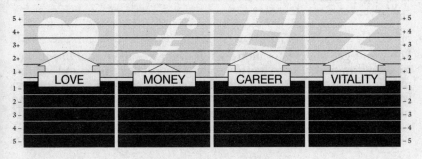

20 MONDAY
Moon Age Day 10 Moon Sign Virgo

am...

pm...

You benefit a great deal today from mixing with as broad a cross-section of people as possible. This is a sociable time and one during which you might also be able to turn your mind towards love and romance. Money matters can be addressed successfully, particularly if you involve family members where appropriate.

21 TUESDAY
Moon Age Day 11 Moon Sign Libra

am...

pm...

As the Moon arrives in your own zodiac sign, you can take advantage of one of the best days of the month for putting new plans into action, and for coming to terms with the changes your life really needs. Confidence shouldn't be lacking, and neither is a little cheek! Why not persuade friends to help you out?

22 WEDNESDAY
Moon Age Day 12 Moon Sign Libra

am...

pm...

The lunar high continues, highlighting your willingness to make ground in projects old and new. High spirits are the order of the day, even if you are mixing with people who really could do with a more active sense of humour. If anyone can brighten them up at this time, that person is you.

23 THURSDAY
Moon Age Day 13 Moon Sign Scorpio

am...

pm...

You won't get what you want from this day if you allow your impatience to show too much. It's vital to create a good impression, and for this reason your attitude towards others is very important. Even if you feel frustrated by circumstances, you need to smile and to maintain a state of equilibrium.

24 FRIDAY
Moon Age Day 14 Moon Sign Scorpio

am ....

pm..

Trends suggest it might not be easy to make personal relationships work out exactly as you would wish. You can't expect everyone to fall into line, and sometimes you simply have to accept that you won't persuade others to adopt your rational point of view. It might be best to stick with friends for the moment.

25 SATURDAY
Moon Age Day 15 Moon Sign Sagittarius

am ....

pm..

This would be an excellent time to seek the wide blue yonder. Libra has its restless spells, and there are indications that this could be one of them. Sticking to what you know can be quite boring. Taking a few chances would be no bad thing, though you need to ensure that risks are calculated ones, at least for now.

26 SUNDAY
Moon Age Day 16 Moon Sign Sagittarius

am ....

pm..

Cultural matters give you scope to show your best side and to demonstrate the more intellectual qualities within your Libran nature. You might decide to spend your Sunday doing a variety of different things, but 'variety' is definitely the key word here. Keep a sense of proportion if you are out and about tonight.

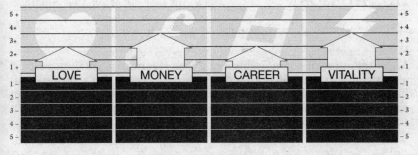

27 MONDAY
Moon Age Day 17 Moon Sign Capricorn

am...

pm...

It's one thing to be eager for professional success, but things won't always turn out quite the way you would wish. Take life steadily and look for opportunities in places where others fail to see them. Confidence is available, but might be buried below the surface for most of the day. Why not seek some reassurance?

28 TUESDAY
Moon Age Day 18 Moon Sign Capricorn

am...

pm...

There are newer and broader horizons on offer, even if you can't make use of them early on. It's time to ensure that even people you don't know too well can understand what you are about. On the other hand, you might find it more difficult to see right through to the heart of some matters in the way you normally do.

29 WEDNESDAY
Moon Age Day 19 Moon Sign Aquarius

am...

pm...

Even if you are willing to meet with people today, and quite able to speak your mind, that's no guarantee that everything will go entirely your way. Be patient, keep your cool and don't react to provocation. Remember these pieces of advice and you stand a chance of winning through in the end.

30 THURSDAY
Moon Age Day 20 Moon Sign Aquarius

am...

pm...

Make the most of a continuing high with regard to mental interests of almost any sort. Be willing to look again at old issues that return to your life, though it's worth doing so with a radically different attitude this time. Money matters are well accented, and there are gains to be made in some quite unexpected places.

31 FRIDAY
Moon Age Day 21 Moon Sign Aquarius

am ....

pm...

The competitive side of your nature is to the fore today, though whether you can put this trend to good use remains in some doubt. Constant attention to detail is probably not something that would interest you too much today. A broad overview of life works much better, in almost every sphere.

1 SATURDAY
Moon Age Day 22 Moon Sign Pisces

am ....

pm...

This is the start of a short period during which there's a risk you will take yourself for granted. Even if you spend much of your time supporting others, you have the right to think about your own life too. There's nothing wrong with allowing others to work on your behalf somewhat more than has been the case for a while.

2 SUNDAY
Moon Age Day 23 Moon Sign Pisces

am ....

pm...

Would you prefer to stay away from the deeper, more introspective aspects of life at the moment? Nevertheless, you need to be ready to respond if they rise to the surface, perhaps as a result of the behaviour and attitudes of others. Conforming to expectations might not be very easy right now.

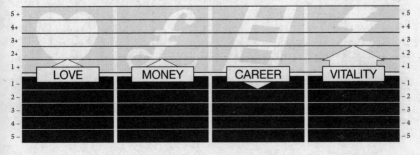

June

2013

YOUR MONTH AT A GLANCE

$\oplus$ = Opportunities are around $\ominus$ = Be on the defensive   ⬤ = Life is pretty ordinary

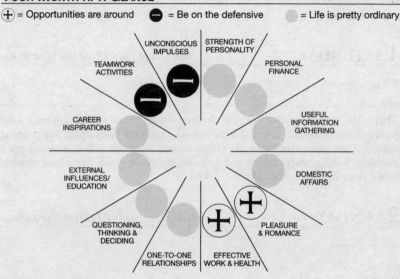

STRENGTH OF PERSONALITY

UNCONSCIOUS IMPULSES

TEAMWORK ACTIVITIES

PERSONAL FINANCE

CAREER INSPIRATIONS

USEFUL INFORMATION GATHERING

EXTERNAL INFLUENCES/ EDUCATION

DOMESTIC AFFAIRS

QUESTIONING, THINKING & DECIDING

PLEASURE & ROMANCE

ONE-TO-ONE RELATIONSHIPS

EFFECTIVE WORK & HEALTH

JUNE HIGHS AND LOWS

Here I show you how the rhythms of the Moon will affect you this month. Like the tide, your energies and abilities will rise and fall with its pattern. When it is above the centre line, go for it, when it is below, you should be resting.

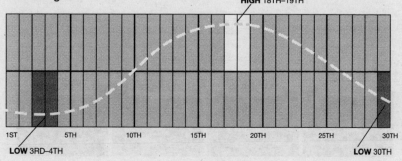

HIGH 18TH–19TH

1ST   5TH   10TH   15TH   20TH   25TH   30TH

LOW 3RD–4TH

LOW 30TH

3 MONDAY
Moon Age Day 24 Moon Sign Aries

am ....

pm ....

Practical matters could be difficult to control as the lunar low arrives. You might even decide that there isn't too much point in trying. Opt for a social sort of day and one during which you have a chance to chat freely with as many different people as possible. That might include someone you haven't seen for a while.

4 TUESDAY
Moon Age Day 25 Moon Sign Aries

am ....

pm ....

Once again this is probably not an ideal period to pursue self-gain. On the contrary, confidence could be distinctly lacking. At least this trend should dissuade you from going overboard in terms of your opinion of yourself. By tomorrow you have everything you need to get yourself back on form again.

5 WEDNESDAY
Moon Age Day 26 Moon Sign Taurus

am ....

pm ....

Trends indicate the potential for minor conflicts around at present, perhaps within the family. It pays to stay away from these if you can and certainly don't allow yourself to become too deeply involved. When dealing with others it would be sensible to look for some way to strike a happy medium in discussions.

6 THURSDAY
Moon Age Day 27 Moon Sign Taurus

am ....

pm ....

Work matters continue to offer you scope to make this a productive interlude, and even if you are not pushing ahead quite as well as you might wish, there shouldn't be a great deal to hold you back. Creating just the right atmosphere to make others feel comfortable should be a natural aspect of life now.

7 FRIDAY
Moon Age Day 28 Moon Sign Taurus

am...

pm...

You need to be aware of powerful ego tendencies now, and take care not to overstate your case. This is particularly true if you are dealing with sensitive types or people you know take offence all too easily. Be ready to deal with issues in your relationships with older family members later.

8 SATURDAY
Moon Age Day 0 Moon Sign Gemini

am...

pm...

Your need for personal freedom and the requirements that other people have of you could now be the source of conflict. As long as you retain your good-natured optimism you can ensure that all is well. Flexibility is the name of the game when it comes to dealing with specific arrangements or travel plans.

9 SUNDAY
Moon Age Day 1 Moon Sign Gemini

am...

pm...

Differing aspects of communication come under the spotlight on this Sunday. Face-to-face contacts have the most positive potential, and so getting out of the house on visits is a viable option. What might be less successful is settling for a day that is based entirely on expectations and routines you can do without.

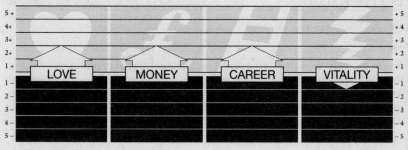

10 MONDAY
Moon Age Day 2 Moon Sign Cancer

am ....

pm ....

There is now a firm emphasis on the practical world. That might encourage you to put home-based matters on the back burner, at least for a while. If your patterns of work are changing, try to be flexible and to make the most of the situation. Romance is well accented at the moment, and it could come from some unexpected directions.

11 TUESDAY
Moon Age Day 3 Moon Sign Cancer

am ....

pm ....

You can capitalise on a real winning streak now in more ways than one. Not only do you have what it takes to make a very good impression on others, you can also reap the benefits of what they offer you in return. Watch that ego, though, because you need to avoid letting those around you think you are lording it over them.

12 WEDNESDAY
Moon Age Day 4 Moon Sign Cancer

am ....

pm ....

There is now a strong emphasis on friendly communication, brought about as a result of interacting planets in your solar chart. Thinking big becomes possible, though your attitude should always be tempered with a shot of humility. Once again it's a question of making sure others don't get the wrong impression.

13 THURSDAY
Moon Age Day 5 Moon Sign Leo

am ....

pm ....

An ideal time to pursue your search for the odd or unusual in life. Listen to your intuition and react according to its advice. You are in a position to gain support from the most unlikely sources, and to persuade others to put themselves out on your behalf. Your previous kindness has a part to play in this process.

14 FRIDAY
Moon Age Day 6 Moon Sign Leo

am ....

pm..

Trends encourage you to bring to fruition the plans you made a long time ago. Don't be surprised if you manage to get everything happening at the same time. Fortunately you have good endurance at present, which is just as well because this is unlikely to be a particularly restful Sunday for most Libran subjects.

15 SATURDAY
Moon Age Day 7 Moon Sign Virgo

am ....

pm..

If there are forces around today that seem to undermine your strengths, you will simply have to deal with them in the best way you can. Try to avoid getting yourself wound up about things, and rely on the help and support that you can obtain from those around you. Make the most of the goodwill that is on offer now.

16 SUNDAY
Moon Age Day 8 Moon Sign Virgo

am ....

pm..

Bringing matters to a head today is fine, though it's important to think carefully before you commit yourself to a specific course of action. Your strength lies in your ability to see clearly in the direction you should be going, and in your refusal to be diverted from your chosen path. Romance is emphasised in the evening.

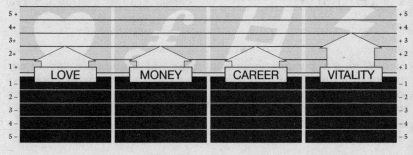

17 MONDAY

Moon Age Day 9 Moon Sign Virgo

am ....

pm...

New gains start to become available. The present position of Mercury is especially useful when it comes to communicating with others. Try not to sit around and think about things too much right now. Bear in mind that you might actually be worrying about matters that have no real significance in the longer term.

18 TUESDAY

Moon Age Day 10 Moon Sign Libra

am ....

pm...

The lunar high brings great opportunities to make gains. Even if you aren't completely satisfied with your level of progress, you certainly have it within you to make the best possible impression. Once you have made up your mind to a particular course of action, there should be no need to let yourself be diverted.

19 WEDNESDAY

Moon Age Day 11 Moon Sign Libra

am ....

pm...

What an excellent time this would be for putting the finishing touches to fresh and innovative ideas. You have what it takes to remain determined and to overthrow obstacles that might normally get in your way. Confidence levels shouldn't be a problem, and there is much to be said for keeping a number of agendas in mind.

20 THURSDAY

Moon Age Day 12 Moon Sign Scorpio

am ....

pm...

It's worth making practical issues your number one priority today, particularly if you have been avoiding them recently. Your powers of communication are to the fore, and this would be an ideal time to put right anything that has been an issue in your life for weeks. Family matters can benefit from positive trends.

21 FRIDAY
Moon Age Day 13 Moon Sign Scorpio

am ....

pm...

You need to find plenty of get-up-and-go today to tackle everything that needs to be done. It pays to keep abreast of local news and events, while at the same time looking carefully at the big picture regarding your own life. A personal approach to family matters would no doubt be appreciated.

22 SATURDAY
Moon Age Day 14 Moon Sign Sagittarius

am ....

pm...

If you feel that pressure is going to upset your judgement today, your best option is to approach all situations slowly and steadily, avoiding unnecessary reactions. You can't expect to get everyone on your side, but when the chips are down there are a number of friends upon whom you can rely.

23 SUNDAY
Moon Age Day 15 Moon Sign Sagittarius

am ....

pm...

There is no doubt that you prefer to live for the moment – that's pretty much the attitude of all the Air signs. However, you also need to realise that some prior planning is necessary, and this fact certainly shouldn't be lost on you today. Keep a sense of proportion regarding situations that crop up later in the day.

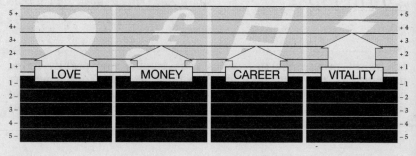

24 MONDAY   *Moon Age Day 16 Moon Sign Capricorn*

am ....

pm..

Maintaining a high profile can assist you to make some positive contacts today, both professionally and on a purely social level. Once again, your need to move around comes under the spotlight, and if you haven't managed much travel yet this year, the call of fresh fields and pastures new may be difficult to counter.

25 TUESDAY   *Moon Age Day 17 Moon Sign Capricorn*

am ....

pm..

Make the most of a potential boost in professional matters, and maybe even a change of job for some Libra subjects. Don't be surprised if you can't obtain help from everyone, because competition is a natural part of life. A day to rise above petty jealousies and ignore any negative influences that are around.

26 WEDNESDAY   *Moon Age Day 18 Moon Sign Aquarius*

am ....

pm..

Being in the know could be as easy as looking into the face of the people you are associating with at present. Your intuition is extremely strong, and this should help you to avoid being fooled by anyone. Be ready to deal with any little mishaps, which are a distinct possibility at the moment.

27 THURSDAY   ☿   *Moon Age Day 19 Moon Sign Aquarius*

am ....

pm..

Once again, you may not find everyone around you to be equally helpful. Bear in mind that people have their motivations, which ought to be easy to guess if you are willing to do a little digging. Confidence is highlighted, and the desire to make changes in and around your home is likely to be fairly strong all day.

28 FRIDAY ☿ *Moon Age Day 20 Moon Sign Pisces*

am ....

pm...

If you are going to appear on a public platform, it's natural to spend time preparing yourself. That's fine, but you need to remember that the spontaneous quality of Libra is also important. There isn't a sign of the zodiac that can 'busk it' better than yours can. If you don't believe this to be true, why not ask a friend?

29 SATURDAY ☿ *Moon Age Day 21 Moon Sign Pisces*

am ....

pm...

Smooth and steady progress should help you to set this Saturday apart, whether or not you are a weekend worker. If you are not committed to practical matters, a trip into the past would be no bad thing. A visit to a museum or gallery could help to feed your intellectual curiosity and your sense of nostalgia.

30 SUNDAY ☿ *Moon Age Day 22 Moon Sign Aries*

am ....

pm...

It's time to take things somewhat slower. The lunar low is upon you now, and other planetary trends could also be exerting an influence on your mood and energy. Even if you have a lot to get done, you would be wise to address it all slowly and steadily, avoiding any tendency to rush things without good cause.

	LOVE		MONEY		CAREER		VITALITY	

July

2013

YOUR MONTH AT A GLANCE

⊕ = Opportunities are around   ⊖ = Be on the defensive   ⬤ = Life is pretty ordinary

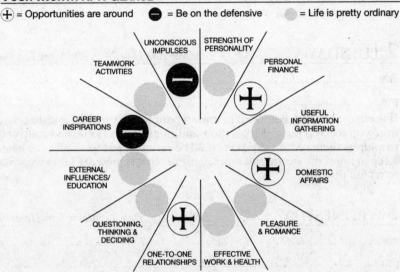

UNCONSCIOUS IMPULSES

STRENGTH OF PERSONALITY

TEAMWORK ACTIVITIES

PERSONAL FINANCE

CAREER INSPIRATIONS

USEFUL INFORMATION GATHERING

EXTERNAL INFLUENCES/ EDUCATION

DOMESTIC AFFAIRS

QUESTIONING, THINKING & DECIDING

PLEASURE & ROMANCE

ONE-TO-ONE RELATIONSHIPS

EFFECTIVE WORK & HEALTH

JULY HIGHS AND LOWS

Here I show you how the rhythms of the Moon will affect you this month. Like the tide, your energies and abilities will rise and fall with its pattern. When it is above the centre line, go for it, when it is below, you should be resting.

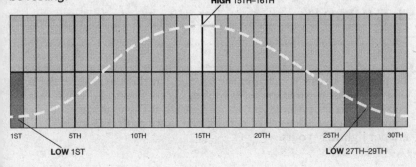

HIGH 15TH–16TH

1ST   5TH   10TH   15TH   20TH   25TH   30TH

LOW 1ST

LOW 27TH–29TH

1 MONDAY ☿ *Moon Age Day 23 Moon Sign Aries*

am...

pm...

Do you feel that something is missing from your life at the start of July? Perhaps the unusual planetary influences that surround you presently have something to do with it. It's important to carry on with your regular routines and don't allow yourself to be thwarted by matters that are not worth worrying about.

2 TUESDAY ☿ *Moon Age Day 24 Moon Sign Taurus*

am...

pm...

If there is one thing you need to know about today's trends, it is that they urge you to keep busy. With a thousand things to be done, and only you to address them specifically, you could be racing about from pillar to post. Keep in mind the steady and serene attitude that represents Libra working to its full potential.

3 WEDNESDAY ☿ *Moon Age Day 25 Moon Sign Taurus*

am...

pm...

Pushing ahead on most fronts gives you an opportunity to make a very positive and memorable impression. There's nothing wrong with nostalgic moments, as long as you don't get obsessed with the past. Most of the really important aspects of your life still lie ahead of you. You can reach out and touch them soon.

4 THURSDAY ☿ *Moon Age Day 26 Moon Sign Taurus*

am...

pm...

Be prepared to put yourself in the limelight at this time. Make the most of a real boost to your spirits, even if this is coming from within. Even if you can't get everything you want from life at the moment, you should come quite close. Beware of getting tied down with responsibilities that are not rightfully yours.

5 FRIDAY ☿ *Moon Age Day 27 Moon Sign Gemini*

am ....

pm..

Career matters are still well accented as the working week draws to an end for most of you. In some ways you could be slowing down, but that's not surprising if you've been maintaining a hectic pace of late. There are good reasons to focus on travel, and on the possibility of seeing people you haven't met for a while.

6 SATURDAY ☿ *Moon Age Day 28 Moon Sign Gemini*

am ....

pm..

There are signs that crowds might hold little appeal at present, and you can afford to be much more at ease with your own company. This doesn't mean this has to be a dull day. Far from it, if you make sure you keep busy. Minor complications are possible in relationships, but these merely add to the general spice of life.

7 SUNDAY ☿ *Moon Age Day 0 Moon Sign Cancer*

am ....

pm..

Professionally you can make the most of the progressive astrological trends that surround you at this time. Information you obtain today could help you to plan more easily and to attract help and support from interested parties. Socially you should be on top form and willing to make a good impression on those around you.

5 +			+ 5
4+			+ 4
3+			+ 3
2+			+ 2
1 +			+ 1
LOVE	MONEY	CAREER	VITALITY
1 -			- 1
2 -			- 2
3 -			- 3
4 -			- 4
5 -			- 5

101

8 MONDAY ☿ *Moon Age Day 1 Moon Sign Cancer*

am ....

pm ....

Discussions with authority figures could help you to achieve some genuine advances now. Be a little careful over what you consume, because trends suggest that stomach problems may be a distinct possibility. For some Librans this is a time of contemplation and regrouping. A few hours thinking can work wonders later.

9 TUESDAY ☿ *Moon Age Day 2 Moon Sign Cancer*

am ....

pm ....

A winding up of certain projects and periods in your life merely allows you to open the door to new ones. That's what this part of the week is all about. There is no time to allow yourself to be stuck in any sort of rut, and you can achieve the very most when you are willing to join in with any fun that is going on around you.

10 WEDNESDAY ☿ *Moon Age Day 3 Moon Sign Leo*

am ....

pm ....

The spotlight is now on people who come new and fresh into your life. This is something that you should encourage, though time-served friends also deserve a slice of your attention. By all means seek opinions from others about your general appearance, but that doesn't mean you should allow them to alter your originality.

11 THURSDAY ☿ *Moon Age Day 4 Moon Sign Leo*

am ....

pm ....

Although you might now have less scope for influencing those around you, you can still enjoy what the day has to offer in a general sense. You can afford to turn your mind to offbeat and odd interests. Bear in mind that it might be difficult for some of your friends to follow you down certain paths.

12 FRIDAY ☿ *Moon Age Day 5 Moon Sign Virgo*

am ....

pm..

A few delays are possible in terms of professional matters, but you can ensure that the same is not true in a personal or social sense. It's time to focus your attention on having fun and on serving the needs of the people you care for the most. It pays to consider the requirements of family members in particular now.

13 SATURDAY ☿ *Moon Age Day 6 Moon Sign Virgo*

am ....

pm..

The home bird in you begins to make a temporary appearance. Why not? It's one of the most promising months of the year weather-wise, and you should be able to find plenty to do around the house and garden. If you decide to get out and about, a shopping trip would be ideal, because you have what it takes to sniff out a real bargain now.

14 SUNDAY ☿ *Moon Age Day 7 Moon Sign Virgo*

am ....

pm..

Be as organised as possible today and don't allow yourself to be bamboozled into situations that are not of your own choosing. There are indications that finances might be rather variable at the moment, but it's up to you to recognise that the most important things in life won't cost you a single penny now.

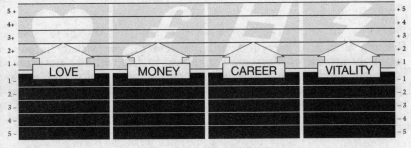

15 MONDAY ☿ *Moon Age Day 8 Moon Sign Libra*

am...

pm...

Rely on your intuitive insight, which suddenly comes to the fore as the Moon surges into your zodiac sign. When the lunar high comes at the start of a summer week, the prognosis has to be positive. All you must remember today is that you won't make full use of your potential by sitting around and doing nothing.

16 TUESDAY ☿ *Moon Age Day 9 Moon Sign Libra*

am...

pm...

Definitely a time to strike while the iron is hot. The Moon is still on your side and Librans have potential to make this a week to remember. Conversation works best if you are articulate and can find the right words to express your opinions. Why not seek help from friends, and at the same time, enjoy their company?

17 WEDNESDAY ☿ *Moon Age Day 10 Moon Sign Scorpio*

am...

pm...

Attention needs to be focused on your own needs today. Being selfish is far from typical Libran behaviour, but there are times when it is necessary. Nevertheless, you have what it takes to entertain others on the way, and to make new friends, almost without any effort at all.

18 THURSDAY ☿ *Moon Age Day 11 Moon Sign Scorpio*

am...

pm...

Keeping abreast of everything that happens in your vicinity is quite important now. Even if you are keeping up to date with necessary jobs, you might have the feeling that there is more and more to do. It is possible that you are panicking unnecessarily. Maybe you need to stand back and look at matters from a distance.

19 FRIDAY
☿ *Moon Age Day 12 Moon Sign Sagittarius*

am...

pm...

Your power to attract just the right sort of people into your life has seldom been more noteworthy than is the case now. It pays to get any urgent jobs out of the way as quickly as you can. Once you have done so, the time is right to socialise as much as possible. Contacts you make at the moment can be important.

20 SATURDAY
☿ *Moon Age Day 13 Moon Sign Sagittarius*

am...

pm...

Along comes a time during which you have scope to seek new experiences. All day long your mind should be working, even if you are still committed to the routines of everyday life. It has to be said that this would be one of the most fortunate periods of the year for Libra to take a holiday.

21 SUNDAY
Moon Age Day 14 Moon Sign Capricorn

am...

pm...

Keep life as varied as you can and don't allow yourself to be pushed into a form of drudgery that really isn't your thing at present. They say that variety is the spice of life, and that is certainly the case for Libra now. The emphasis is on living exclusively for the moment, so making long-term plans probably won't appeal.

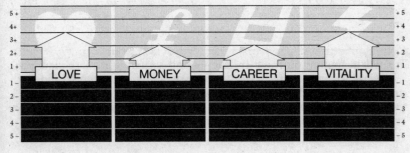

22 MONDAY
Moon Age Day 15 Moon Sign Capricorn

am...

pm...

Monday brings a sense of movement and change into your life, once again stimulated by the position of the Sun. An active and enterprising approach is the order of the day, and this helps you to please everyone as much as you can, while retaining your own sense of independence. It's a lot to ask, but you can manage it!

23 TUESDAY
Moon Age Day 16 Moon Sign Aquarius

am...

pm...

There's nothing wrong with finding people around who can help you with your ambitions today. All you have to do is look carefully and maybe ask a few leading questions. In a more personal sense, you can't expect everyone to have your best interests at heart. If someone has it in for you, consider if this may be because they are jealous.

24 WEDNESDAY
Moon Age Day 17 Moon Sign Aquarius

am...

pm...

Be prepared to box clever and use some friendly persuasion with colleagues in order to make progress at work. Even if you choose to make this a quieter interlude than would normally be the case, this will at least allow you time think, and possibly come up with answers that might otherwise pass you by in busier moments.

25 THURSDAY
Moon Age Day 18 Moon Sign Pisces

am...

pm...

It's worth finding out how colleagues and superiors at work view your efforts at the moment. If you've been working consistently and with great enthusiasm during this year, you should have certainly created a positive impression. Many Librans could feel inspired to seek greater responsibilities between now and the autumn.

26 FRIDAY
Moon Age Day 19 Moon Sign Pisces

am ....

pm...

An ideal day to address personal concerns and wishes. The position of little Mercury indicates the need to be alert for the possibility of important communications arriving any time now. When it comes to alterations you have been considering making at home, bear in mind that delays are likely, although they are probably necessary.

27 SATURDAY
Moon Age Day 20 Moon Sign Aries

am ....

pm...

With the lunar low around, you have an opportunity now to review specific elements of your life and to put them into perspective. You can't expect everyone to have your best interests at heart, though you should be careful not to judge too harshly, either today or tomorrow. Your point of perspective is not neutral.

28 SUNDAY
Moon Age Day 21 Moon Sign Aries

am ....

pm...

A quiet day is on offer. With the lunar low around this may not be the most exciting Sunday you will ever experience. Not that this matters too much, because you should be happy to simply go with the flow. When it comes to journeys of any sort, there is much to be said for allowing others to deal with the arrangements.

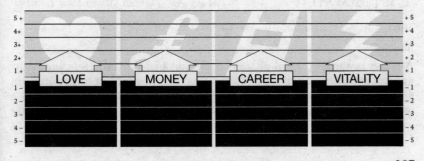

29 MONDAY *Moon Age Day 22 Moon Sign Aries*

am...

pm...

Get as much rest as you can and avoid pushing yourself too much. In a sense, it doesn't matter how hard you work because it won't be easy to get ahead whilst the Moon is in your opposite zodiac sign. It would be far better to stand and look at certain elements of life from a sensible distance.

30 TUESDAY *Moon Age Day 23 Moon Sign Taurus*

am...

pm...

A brand new phase is under way, offering some real highlights. The Sun is now in your eleventh house and you have scope to create some summer fun. All group and teamwork issues are positively accented, as are friendships and some quite startling encounters with members of the opposite sex!

31 WEDNESDAY *Moon Age Day 24 Moon Sign Taurus*

am...

pm...

Today has potential to offer useful opportunities on the work front. With more energy available and a return of your accustomed optimism, you can push forward progressively, and with a much fairer attitude. Librans who are not working today could look at jobs that need addressing in and around the home.

1 THURSDAY *Moon Age Day 25 Moon Sign Gemini*

am...

pm...

A rather rewarding social phase is now available. With the Sun presently occupying your solar eleventh house, you are in a position to get on with a whole variety of different individuals. In new ventures it is important to keep a sense of proportion, even if people around you are failing to do so.

2 FRIDAY   *Moon Age Day 26 Moon Sign Gemini*

am ....

pm..

Although today could be demanding, you can also ensure that it is rewarding. You will need to do whatever you are involved in to the very best of your ability. Sporting prowess is well accented, a fact that should interest Librans who are keen to pit themselves against others in a competitive way.

3 SATURDAY   *Moon Age Day 27 Moon Sign Gemini*

am ....

pm..

There is much to be said for putting personal and domestic issues on hold, whilst you choose to get on with something practical. Weekend-working Librans are encouraged to put in that extra bit of effort right now, but the results ought to be more than worthwhile. A day to keep up your efforts socially.

4 SUNDAY   *Moon Age Day 28 Moon Sign Cancer*

am ....

pm..

Your capacity for clear-headed judgement has rarely been better. In addition, current planetary trends assist you to make short work of even difficult or challenging tasks. Handing out advice is all very well, but be careful in what direction you are offering it. You should definitely avoid playing 'piggy in the middle'.

August

2013

Your Month at a Glance

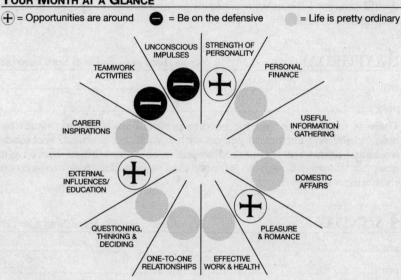

(+) = Opportunities are around   — = Be on the defensive   = Life is pretty ordinary

UNCONSCIOUS IMPULSES

STRENGTH OF PERSONALITY

TEAMWORK ACTIVITIES

PERSONAL FINANCE

CAREER INSPIRATIONS

USEFUL INFORMATION GATHERING

EXTERNAL INFLUENCES/ EDUCATION

DOMESTIC AFFAIRS

QUESTIONING, THINKING & DECIDING

PLEASURE & ROMANCE

ONE-TO-ONE RELATIONSHIPS

EFFECTIVE WORK & HEALTH

August Highs and Lows

Here I show you how the rhythms of the Moon will affect you this month. Like the tide, your energies and abilities will rise and fall with its pattern. When it is above the centre line, go for it, when it is below, you should be resting.

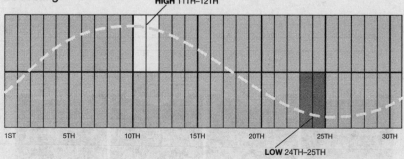

HIGH 11TH–12TH

1ST   5TH   10TH   15TH   20TH   25TH   30TH

LOW 24TH–25TH

5 MONDAY

Moon Age Day 29 Moon Sign Cancer

am ....

pm..

The continuing boost to social possibilities presently coming from the Sun assists you to be the life and soul of any party. This is an excellent time for travel and for dealing with outstanding jobs that need a very special touch. Your ability to address any sort of boredom counts for a great deal at present.

6 TUESDAY

Moon Age Day 0 Moon Sign Leo

am ....

pm..

Group-related issues are once more to the fore. These shouldn't be difficult for you with your easy-going Air-sign ways. Today works best if you get any important work out of the way as early as you can. If you manage to do so you leave yourself with some hours later that can be dedicated to simply having fun.

7 WEDNESDAY

Moon Age Day 1 Moon Sign Leo

am ....

pm..

Work issues could end up in a state of disarray if you don't get yourself organised. Be willing to call upon the help and support of a genuine professional or someone who has a type of knowledge you don't. It's a question of finding friendly individuals who are willing to offer you sound counsel.

8 THURSDAY

Moon Age Day 2 Moon Sign Leo

am ....

pm..

Tasks requiring serious concentration could suffer if you allow your mind to wander today. Instead of making a mess of things, why not leave some of the requirements until later? You can afford to focus on making sure others realise how important they are to you, and enjoying the cut and thrust of the world at large.

9 FRIDAY
Moon Age Day 3 Moon Sign Virgo

am...

pm...

What you learn when involved in group situations is the most important information of all. Use every morsel of gossip that you can find, and be prepared to turn half an idea into a cast-iron notion. Planning ahead is favoured, and particularly so when it comes to anything involving cash or a change of location.

10 SATURDAY
Moon Age Day 4 Moon Sign Virgo

am...

pm...

A period of minor gains in and around home is on offer this weekend. If, on the other hand, you are ready for a bit of jet-setting, the auspices for travel are equally positive. The outdoor life could certainly appeal, even if that only means doing a bit of weeding, or giving the lawn a haircut!

11 SUNDAY
Moon Age Day 5 Moon Sign Libra

am...

pm...

Make sure all the stops are out! A mental and physical peak is available, and your extra zest for life should do you credit. Don't ignore the needs of loved ones. This is your chance to take them by the hand and drag them off wherever you decide to go. If you have a favourite location, going there today can work wonders.

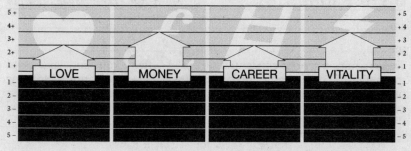

12 MONDAY
Moon Age Day 6 Moon Sign Libra

am ....

pm..

The lunar high now assists you to capitalise on some unexpected favours. If these achieve nothing else, they can at least tend to stimulate your faith in human nature. Just about everything in the garden is coming up roses, and you can afford to spend more time and money on those projects you know to be important.

13 TUESDAY
Moon Age Day 7 Moon Sign Scorpio

am ....

pm..

There are gains to be made through keeping as busy as possible today. If this has seemed to be a very stop–start sort of month, that's all the more reason to react to the more positive moments. Refuse to be sidelined in discussions and insist on having your say. You will earn more respect from others for doing so.

14 WEDNESDAY
Moon Age Day 8 Moon Sign Scorpio

am ....

pm..

It's natural to gravitate towards those with whom you are getting on particularly well, though you need to ask whether you are being taken for a ride. It's important today to stick to those people who you have known for a long time. It will be difficult to make too many gains at work, or indeed in practical situations.

15 THURSDAY
Moon Age Day 9 Moon Sign Scorpio

am ....

pm..

This is a day when you have the ability to talk anyone into just about anything. Even if you start the day feeling rather hesitant, it shouldn't last long. This would be an ideal time to plan a special occasion of some kind with a loved one. Words of love come naturally under present influences.

16 FRIDAY
Moon Age Day 10 Moon Sign Sagittarius

am ....

pm ....

Trends suggest a slightly taxing element for today, and concentration is called for. You need to focus on the demands that are made on both your time and your energy, and realise that not everyone you come across is going help you out. Today could be an exception in a period that is generally highly sociable.

17 SATURDAY
Moon Age Day 11 Moon Sign Sagittarius

am ....

pm ....

Be willing to take a patient approach with the people who mean the most to you. You can't expect everyone to do things your way for now, and you need to be aware that alternatives are possible and that they may lead to the same destination. Speaking of destinations, this is another favourable time to think about journeys.

18 SUNDAY
Moon Age Day 12 Moon Sign Capricorn

am ....

pm ....

If there are difficulties regarding emotional ties, maybe you need to stand back and look at the situation from a distance. Getting too involved in discussions that could so easily turn into rows isn't to be recommended. You will do yourself a favour if you keep most contacts light and even superficial for now.

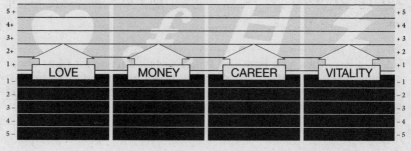

19 MONDAY   *Moon Age Day 13 Moon Sign Capricorn*

am ....

pm..

Although you have what it takes to make great strides at work, it is through friendship that you can show your most positive qualities. There is nothing immoral about making use of your current popularity, particularly if you are able to offer happiness to those around you.

20 TUESDAY   *Moon Age Day 14 Moon Sign Aquarius*

am ....

pm..

Getting ahead in life right now is just as much about charm and personality as it is about really knowing what you are doing. You need to show the true Libran qualities within you this week. Any chance to get away from the normal routines of life should be firmly grasped with both hands.

21 WEDNESDAY   *Moon Age Day 15 Moon Sign Aquarius*

am ....

pm..

Making progress is now a question of accepting help from others, and the process begins today. You needn't turn away from advice, especially if it comes from people who plainly know what they are talking about. It's worth looking for chances to improve your finances, particularly in the afternoon and evening.

22 THURSDAY   *Moon Age Day 16 Moon Sign Pisces*

am ....

pm..

There are gains to be made today, some of them in less than likely directions. With strong social trends prevailing, you can afford to make the most of the summer weather to mix with friends, as well as some people you don't know at all yet. Be prepared to elicit some very striking compliments!

23 FRIDAY
Moon Age Day 17 Moon Sign Pisces

am ....

pm ....

Personal ambitions need to be carefully focused, though with the lunar low immediately before you, the chance of actually getting much done in a concrete sense may not be high. The key advice for today is to avoid getting involved in conflicts, especially those that had nothing to do with you in the first place.

24 SATURDAY
Moon Age Day 18 Moon Sign Aries

am ....

pm ....

Try as you may, there may be no escaping the feeling that others are getting ahead more than you are. Ignore this mood and simply set out to have a rewarding weekend. As long as you don't bite off more than you can chew and are willing to relax, you can keep things on track. Once again, rows are best avoided.

25 SUNDAY
Moon Age Day 19 Moon Sign Aries

am ....

pm ....

Even if you still aren't able to make a great deal of headway, the fog should start to clear somewhat as the day advances. Keep an open mind about domestic issues, and beware of dismissing possibilities until you have at least looked at them fairly. Why not make time for a romantic interlude later in the day?

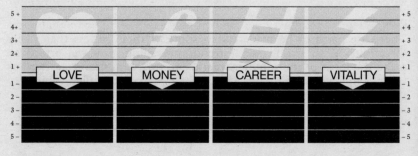

26 MONDAY
Moon Age Day 20 Moon Sign Taurus

am ....

pm...

This is not a day during which you are encouraged to seek too much in the way of responsibility. Better by far to find some enjoyment for yourself, and best of all if you could arrange to take a break. There are signs that your old friend, wanderlust, could be paying you a visit at any time now.

27 TUESDAY
Moon Age Day 21 Moon Sign Taurus

am ....

pm...

Even if your mind is working quickly enough at present, there is a distinct possibility that your body is refusing to keep up. Your power to influence situations could be somewhat diminished, and you may be tempted to rely heavily on others. If you've helped them out in the past, that seems like a fair exchange.

28 WEDNESDAY
Moon Age Day 22 Moon Sign Gemini

am ....

pm...

The Sun is now in your solar twelfth house, offering you a more contemplative interlude than is likely to have been the case in recent weeks. This is a time to think things through, before the more hectic spell when the Sun enters your first house in three weeks or so. Don't be in too much of a rush to achieve objectives.

29 THURSDAY
Moon Age Day 23 Moon Sign Gemini

am ....

pm...

Almost any exchange of ideas can prove to be both useful and enjoyable today. The talkative side of your nature is emphasised – big time – and you should be able to make a favourable impression, even on people you thought didn't like you too much. Be prepared to find humour in confusing situations.

30 FRIDAY
Moon Age Day 24   Moon Sign Gemini

am...

pm...

This is an ideal time for tackling joint financial issues. That's fine if you are in the mood, but that might not necessarily be the case right now. Do you feel you have to compete for the attention of loved ones? That might mean turning off the television set and throwing away the remote control!

31 SATURDAY
Moon Age Day 25   Moon Sign Cancer

am...

pm...

Although the general advice today would be 'don't try to please everybody', whether you choose to follow it is another matter. The fact is that you love to get on with the world at large. Often, if this proves difficult, there's a temptation to blame yourself. Such an attitude simply would not be fair at present.

1 SUNDAY
Moon Age Day 26   Moon Sign Cancer

am...

pm...

Be ready to deal with a few pitfalls at the start of this week, which are influenced by the current position of the Moon. The trend is very short-lived and need not prevent you from getting on in a general sense. Keep a sense of proportion, even if you are dealing with people who don't appear to have a sense of humour.

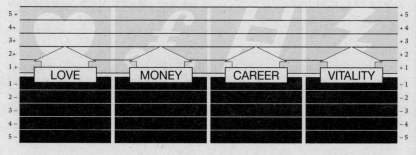

September 2013

YOUR MONTH AT A GLANCE

⊕ = Opportunities are around　　● = Be on the defensive　　● = Life is pretty ordinary

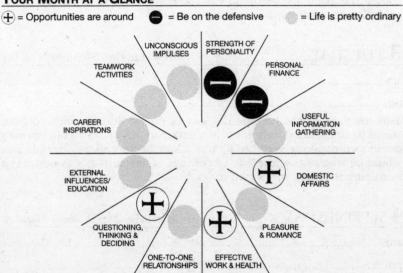

- UNCONSCIOUS IMPULSES
- STRENGTH OF PERSONALITY (−)
- PERSONAL FINANCE (−)
- TEAMWORK ACTIVITIES
- USEFUL INFORMATION GATHERING
- CAREER INSPIRATIONS
- DOMESTIC AFFAIRS (+)
- EXTERNAL INFLUENCES/ EDUCATION
- QUESTIONING, THINKING & DECIDING (+)
- PLEASURE & ROMANCE
- ONE-TO-ONE RELATIONSHIPS
- EFFECTIVE WORK & HEALTH (+)

SEPTEMBER HIGHS AND LOWS

Here I show you how the rhythms of the Moon will affect you this month. Like the tide, your energies and abilities will rise and fall with its pattern. When it is above the centre line, go for it, when it is below, you should be resting.

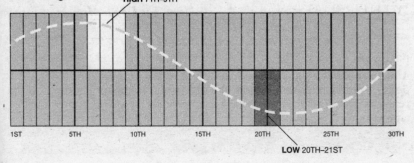

HIGH 7TH–9TH

1ST　　5TH　　10TH　　15TH　　20TH　　25TH　　30TH

LOW 20TH–21ST

119

2 MONDAY
Moon Age Day 27 Moon Sign Leo

am ....

pm ....

You might have little choice but to give way to certain emotions now. Perhaps that's no bad thing, because at least it helps you to let others know where they stand. Confidence might not be high, but when it comes to making up your mind you certainly shouldn't be left out in the cold. You are more capable now than you believe.

3 TUESDAY
Moon Age Day 28 Moon Sign Leo

am ....

pm ....

This has potential to become the sort of period during which you can afford to sit back and look at life in a detached manner. This opportunity doesn't come along very often, and it can be very useful indeed. You would be wise not to give way to cravings of any sort. It's a question of remaining in charge of yourself today.

4 WEDNESDAY
Moon Age Day 0 Moon Sign Leo

am ....

pm ....

A minor but important boost to your love life should be coming along today. Getting on with people is rarely difficult for you but should be especially easy right now. In any project that takes deep thought you won't excel for the moment. Superficiality is part of the present planetary line-up.

5 THURSDAY
Moon Age Day 1 Moon Sign Virgo

am ....

pm ....

The need to keep things in good working order is paramount today. This doesn't simply refer to mechanical gadgets of one sort or another, but to relationships as well. If you have been ignoring a particular individual of late, you need to acknowledge this, and then start to put it right.

6 FRIDAY
Moon Age Day 2 Moon Sign Virgo

am ....

pm...

Tolerance and understanding towards loved ones can make all the difference today. Normally this wouldn't be a problem, unless you feel as if you have been held back rather more than you would have wished of late. All the same, you need to have a listening ear and be ready with some timely advice.

7 SATURDAY
Moon Age Day 3 Moon Sign Libra

am ....

pm...

High spirits prevail with the arrival of the lunar high, and it appears that you have everything you need to make the best possible impression on a variety of different people. You can afford to stick up for your point of view, but don't be surprised if others don't react. Not everyone is in the mood to cross swords!

8 SUNDAY
Moon Age Day 4 Moon Sign Libra

am ....

pm...

Talking others round to doing things your way really should be a piece of cake under current astrological trends. Make the most of opportunities to strengthen your finances, and utilise the good luck that is on offer. This has potential to be the very best day of the month for doing any form of travelling.

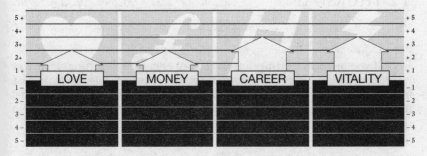

9 MONDAY
Moon Age Day 5 Moon Sign Libra

am ....

pm..

Getting your own way may seem so easy now that you might not bother trying. Certainly, you can afford to put yourself in the limelight, maybe by taking part in some sort of public event. You should have good reason to feel proud of yourself, but even more so of younger family members or friends.

10 TUESDAY
Moon Age Day 6 Moon Sign Scorpio

am ....

pm..

Discussions of any sort are now favoured, since trends highlight your ability to put your message across. It pays to get on with things today because the more you achieve at the moment, the greater the amount of time you will have to spend on yourself later. Help can be sought in some interesting directions.

11 WEDNESDAY
Moon Age Day 7 Moon Sign Scorpio

am ....

pm..

A new boost to romance, or at the very least a continuation of recent positive events in this sphere, is the continuing gift of Venus. This is a Wednesday that you definitely have scope to enjoy, and it brings with it the potential for you to achieve even better things in the remainder of the week. Don't settle for second-best.

12 THURSDAY
Moon Age Day 8 Moon Sign Sagittarius

am ....

pm..

Even if you are now putting a great deal of energy into getting what you want from life, it's important to appreciate that people who have limited imagination won't help you to move forward progressively. Be willing to mix with dynamic types, including individuals who can share their own real experiences.

13 FRIDAY
Moon Age Day 9 Moon Sign Sagittarius

am ....

pm..

Be aware that there may be personal challenges and confrontations ahead. The best way to deal with these is one at a time. Worrying won't achieve anything at all, and might only lead to confusion. In any case, it's up to you to discover that many of your worries are completely without foundation.

14 SATURDAY
Moon Age Day 10 Moon Sign Capricorn

am ....

pm..

The spotlight is now on looking and feeling your very best. In addition, your practical abilities are enhanced, as is your capacity to sort out previously awkward situations. Keeping a happy smile on your face for most of the day will demonstrate your positive outlook to others, and assist you to make important allies.

15 SUNDAY
Moon Age Day 11 Moon Sign Capricorn

am ....

pm..

With energy and willpower now on your side, you needn't let anything hold you back. When it comes to getting things done in the practical world, your abilities should be second to none. If the behaviour or attitudes of loved ones are a mystery to you, some gentle questioning should help to put you in the know.

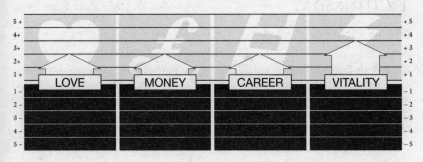

123

16 MONDAY
Moon Age Day 12 Moon Sign Aquarius

am...

pm...

Make sure you are open to new experiences, and be willing to seek them out this week. From the very start, you need to demonstrate that you have plenty of vitality. What really stands out is your ability to communicate with almost anyone. Your ability to tackle routine or tedious jobs now is another matter entirely!

17 TUESDAY
Moon Age Day 13 Moon Sign Aquarius

am...

pm...

A sense of confusion regarding personal matters is something you need to be prepared for at this time. Avoid unnecessary rows, particularly if they concern issues that you don't see as being especially important. The main job for today is to try to get your priorities right. Financial progress is also well marked under current trends.

18 WEDNESDAY
Moon Age Day 14 Moon Sign Pisces

am...

pm...

Don't be afraid to face matters head-on today, even if there are some you would prefer not to address at all. Being brave and plunging in head first is the best way forward, and it should help you to get things sorted out early on. You can then afford to turn your attention towards fun – something that definitely does appeal!

19 THURSDAY
Moon Age Day 15 Moon Sign Pisces

am...

pm...

It's worth considering winding down any particularly ambitious projects right now. Making tremendous headway may not be easy when the Sun is in your solar twelfth house, but that only continues for another day or two. In the meantime, it's a question of looking at most elements of life in an entirely realistic way.

20 FRIDAY
Moon Age Day 16 Moon Sign Aries

am..

pm..

The lunar low heralds a potentially slower time, but in your mind you should already be gearing up for a much more entertaining time later. Even if you have plenty of ideas today, putting some of them into practice may not be easy. Remember that seeking support from friends or colleagues might help you to win through.

21 SATURDAY
Moon Age Day 17 Moon Sign Aries

am..

pm..

Some unexpected obstacles could attend the continuing lunar low. Be ready to respond to alterations, delays or even cancellations, particularly when it comes to planned journeys. A degree of frustration is natural, but it's important to find alternatives without letting the grass grow under your feet.

22 SUNDAY
Moon Age Day 18 Moon Sign Taurus

am..

pm..

Fresh opportunities are available now as the Sun moves into your solar first house. It's time to blow away some of the tedium and lethargy of the last few weeks on a tide of enthusiasm and determination. Now you should begin to realise what you are worth and to use your powers to the full.

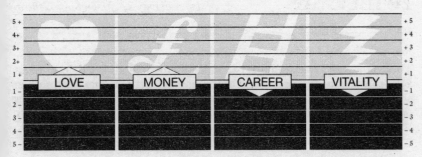

23 MONDAY
Moon Age Day 19 Moon Sign Taurus

am...

pm...

This would not be the best time to hold back when it comes to specific feelings. You can afford to speak your mind and trust that those listening understand your genuine motivations. It isn't usually too difficult for you to get your message across, and current planetary influences give you every encouragement to do this.

24 TUESDAY
Moon Age Day 20 Moon Sign Taurus

am...

pm...

Today offers an opportunity to concentrate on taking independent decisions and to make up your mind regarding medium- and long-term projects. Most important of all is 'now' and the way you are dealing with the various facets of your life. There is much to be said for putting love and romance at the top of your agenda.

25 WEDNESDAY
Moon Age Day 21 Moon Sign Gemini

am...

pm...

You have what it takes to thrive on challenges today, especially professional ones. There are influences around now that encourage you to be like a terrier with a rag, and once you have decided on a specific course of action, you needn't allow anything to change your mind. You need to balance this with flexibility.

26 THURSDAY
Moon Age Day 22 Moon Sign Gemini

am...

pm...

The best way of avoiding any tense atmospheres behind closed doors today is to stay out in the open! In other words, close, personal relationships are more likely to throw up problems. Casual attachments are better for the moment, particularly if you are able to mix with those who make you laugh and stay in a light-hearted mood.

27 FRIDAY

Moon Age Day 23 Moon Sign Cancer

am..

pm..

There are signs that someone from your past could well emerge into your life again at any time now. Even if the memories this stirs are not particularly positive, there are some rewards to be found in this situation. At the very least, it enables you to look at things as they are now and realise how much you have moved on.

28 SATURDAY

Moon Age Day 24 Moon Sign Cancer

am..

pm..

Entertaining the crowds is just one of the options on offer for you today! The really showy qualities of Libra are to the fore, though you shouldn't forget your responsibilities towards family members. By all means assist friends too, though it might be necessary to split your time a good deal.

29 SUNDAY

Moon Age Day 25 Moon Sign Cancer

am..

pm..

You can't rely on luck or believe everything you hear today. Although it is your natural way to trust everyone, you need to bear in mind that there may be people around at the moment who definitely don't have your best interests at heart. Embarking on a new keep-fit campaign would be no bad thing now.

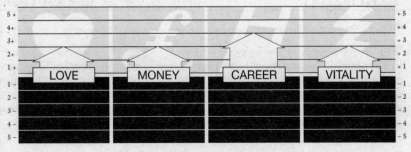

30 MONDAY
Moon Age Day 26 Moon Sign Leo

am ....

pm ....

The best sphere of life today appears to be your career. Taking no for an answer doesn't seem to be an option at present, and your skills of persuasion are definitely highlighted. If you make sure your requests are reasonable, you stand a good chance of convincing others to accommodate them.

1 TUESDAY
Moon Age Day 27 Moon Sign Leo

am ....

pm ....

There is now a change of emphasis as far as your love life is concerned, and you may need to begin doing things in a slightly different way. Even in terms of friendship, variety proves to be the spice of life at this time. There are signs that any recent tendency to ill-health should be clearing up at this time.

2 WEDNESDAY
Moon Age Day 28 Moon Sign Virgo

am ....

pm ....

Venus can offer a boost to finances, though you will have to lend a hand. Keep your eyes open for bargains. This is also a favourable time for selling items you no longer need. Perhaps a rummage through the attic would help? No matter how you go about it, it's time to look for ways to improve your income.

3 THURSDAY
Moon Age Day 29 Moon Sign Virgo

am ....

pm ....

Some hopeful information may now come your way regarding your personal wishes. There is much to be said for putting to one side any matters you have been worrying about and pushing on towards a specific objective. Once again Venus comes to your aid in terms of love. Listen carefully to what people are really saying.

4 FRIDAY

Moon Age Day 0 Moon Sign Virgo

am...

pm..

Making your mind up instantly can be quite rewarding at the moment. This is really no time for standing around and thinking. Everything comes to you when you are decisive and willing to take the lead. Not everyone will want to follow, though the people who matter the most at present probably will.

5 SATURDAY

Moon Age Day 1 Moon Sign Libra

am..

pm..

The best of all worlds is possible today. The Sun is in your solar first house and the Moon is in your zodiac sign. All in all you can make today your own. Go for what you want in life and don't accept any excuses, particularly from yourself. You can capitalise on a real boost to your energy and a tremendous sense of urgency.

6 SUNDAY

Moon Age Day 2 Moon Sign Libra

am..

pm..

At the moment your generosity is to the fore. That's fine, as long as you can afford to lavish money and gifts on others. Where younger family members are concerned you may discover that a little more attention is worth any amount of material gifts. Be willing to confront one or two small fears now.

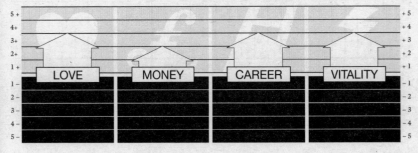

October

2013

Your Month at a Glance

⊕ = Opportunities are around   ⊖ = Be on the defensive   ● = Life is pretty ordinary

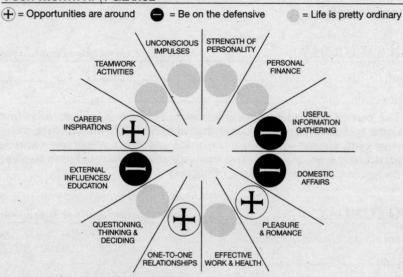

UNCONSCIOUS IMPULSES
STRENGTH OF PERSONALITY
TEAMWORK ACTIVITIES
PERSONAL FINANCE
CAREER INSPIRATIONS ⊕
USEFUL INFORMATION GATHERING ⊖
EXTERNAL INFLUENCES/ EDUCATION ⊖
DOMESTIC AFFAIRS ⊖
QUESTIONING, THINKING & DECIDING
PLEASURE & ROMANCE ⊕
ONE-TO-ONE RELATIONSHIPS ⊕
EFFECTIVE WORK & HEALTH

October Highs and Lows

Here I show you how the rhythms of the Moon will affect you this month. Like the tide, your energies and abilities will rise and fall with its pattern. When it is above the centre line, go for it, when it is below, you should be resting.

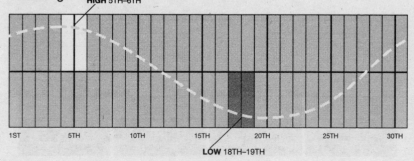

HIGH 5TH–6TH

1ST   5TH   10TH   15TH   20TH   25TH   30TH

LOW 18TH–19TH

7 MONDAY   *Moon Age Day 3 Moon Sign Scorpio*

am ....

pm...

Intimate relationships can now help you to increase your own sense of security, and enable you to feel closer to a particular individual than has been the case for quite some time. Monetary bonuses could also be within your grasp, perhaps coming as a result of efforts that you have put in previously.

8 TUESDAY   *Moon Age Day 4 Moon Sign Scorpio*

am ....

pm...

The sort of information that you can gather via normal conversation could be worth its weight in gold. As a result, this is a day when you really need to pin back your ears and listen. The most mundane form of gossip carries messages that you can turn into a wealth of advantages in the weeks and months ahead.

9 WEDNESDAY   *Moon Age Day 5 Moon Sign Sagittarius*

am ....

pm...

This is a day to enjoy the fruits of some of your past efforts. Even if you feel you are closer than ever to making an important breakthrough in your life, taking a rest would be no bad thing. Make the most of social invitations and any opportunities for love. The only thing to remember is to avoid provoking jealousy in others.

10 THURSDAY   *Moon Age Day 6 Moon Sign Sagittarius*

am ....

pm...

You continue on a roll with all practical matters and should be able to make certain that you are making progress when it comes to work. This doesn't mean that you should slacken your pace. On the contrary, once you have the bit between your teeth you should be pushing onwards and upwards that much harder.

11 FRIDAY

Moon Age Day 7 Moon Sign Capricorn

am...

pm...

In the practical stakes you should once again be achieving plenty right now. If there is something you have wanted to do for a while, but you have shied away from it, now is the time. Prepare to persuade those you hold dearest to give you some useful and even exceptional assistance.

12 SATURDAY

Moon Age Day 8 Moon Sign Capricorn

am...

pm...

There are signs that personal indulgences could come well down your list of priorities today. The emphasis is on the side of your nature that is concerned with looking out for others. If possible, do an extra job right now, giving you time tomorrow to do what you please. Any confusion in relationships can soon be cleared up.

13 SUNDAY

Moon Age Day 9 Moon Sign Aquarius

am...

pm...

Today is an opportunity for you to impress others with both your knowledge and your resilience. Keep up your efforts to get through to difficult types, though not to the extent that you can't make any real practical progress. You can make this a Sunday to remember if you are willing to keep putting in the effort.

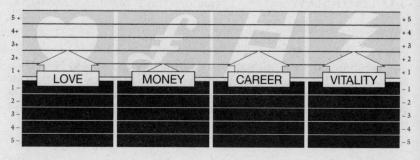

14 MONDAY
Moon Age Day 10 Moon Sign Aquarius

am...

pm...

You have it within you to impress the right sort of people at the beginning of this week. If you are a working Libran you can now afford to take on newer and more demanding responsibilities. Not only can these help you to pep up your professional life, they should offer the chance of some financial rewards.

15 TUESDAY
Moon Age Day 11 Moon Sign Pisces

am...

pm...

It pays to be fired up and ready for challenges at work. You can capitalise on a potentially enterprising and enlightening period, which could include tackling any current relationship problems. You would also be wise to take care over money matters. If deals look too good to be true, they probably are!

16 WEDNESDAY
Moon Age Day 12 Moon Sign Pisces

am...

pm...

Emotional issues and the way you view them could well dominate personal relationships at present, whereas practical matters should be taking centre stage. If you can, defuse issues before they take on any real importance and avoid getting involved in discussions you know could be contentious.

17 THURSDAY
Moon Age Day 13 Moon Sign Pisces

am...

pm...

Trends indicate you could be on a roll at present. Not only can you increase your popularity, you should also be able to use your silver-tongued eloquence to help you get you what you want from life. Nevertheless, you might still be pulled up in your tracks tomorrow, when the lunar low comes along.

18 FRIDAY
Moon Age Day 14 Moon Sign Aries

am ....

pm ....

If you enter this month's lunar low in a very positive frame of mind, you might not even have too much reason to notice its presence. Continue to go for what you want in life generally, though realise that when you shoot for the stars you might only reach the moon. It pays to shun as many rules and regulations as you can.

19 SATURDAY
Moon Age Day 15 Moon Sign Aries

am ....

pm ....

It would probably be a good idea to suspend a few of your efforts for today. The lunar low doesn't necessarily prevent you from getting ahead, though it might make the path somewhat harder to follow. Why not let those around you take the strain while you deliberately choose to take a short break.

20 SUNDAY
Moon Age Day 16 Moon Sign Taurus

am ....

pm ....

There is plenty of initiative available for professional developments under present trends. There's nothing wrong with allowing simple friendship to take something of a back seat at this stage of the week, especially if you are busy with other activities. Caution is the key when it comes to financial matters.

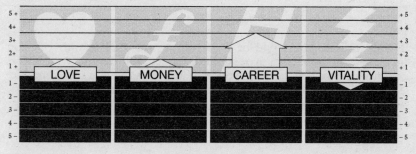

21 MONDAY ☿ *Moon Age Day 17 Moon Sign Taurus*

am ....

pm ....

You have what it takes to attract just the right sort of company today, which means getting on in life, something that is of great importance to you while the Sun occupies its present position in your chart. If you don't manage to find very much time for pleasantries today, you can at least show kindness and compassion.

22 TUESDAY ☿ *Moon Age Day 18 Moon Sign Gemini*

am ....

pm ....

What really sets you apart right now is your ability to speak out in front of others, and to elicit the necessary responses. This is nothing particularly new, but is a quality much enhanced by present planetary trends. In a business sense, you need to be ready to capitalise on new ideas at all stages today.

23 WEDNESDAY ☿ *Moon Age Day 19 Moon Sign Gemini*

am ....

pm ....

You are ready for almost any challenge life can throw at you, plus a few you invent for yourself. All the same, you don't have to go tilting at windmills, just in order to get some excitement into your life. If you haven't enough to do, why not see whether there are people close by who would welcome a helping hand?

24 THURSDAY ☿ *Moon Age Day 20 Moon Sign Gemini*

am ....

pm ....

In money matters, your present ability to think quickly should prove extremely useful. Even if you are not gambling in the generally accepted sense of the word, you might be willing to take a chance that could lead to greater monetary strength further down the line. Make time to enjoy yourself later in the day.

135

25 FRIDAY ☿ *Moon Age Day 21 Moon Sign Cancer*

am...

pm...

The Sun has moved on and now inhabits the second house of your solar chart. For the next three or four weeks you are encouraged to place a stronger emphasis on material possessions than has been the case for the last month. Getting things looking the way you want at home would also suit the present interlude.

26 SATURDAY ☿ *Moon Age Day 22 Moon Sign Cancer*

am...

pm...

There may not be time to do everything you have planned today, but you should at least be determined to try. Confidence remains highlighted, particularly when you are dealing with subject matter that is familiar to you. Your creative potential is especially strong, and you can demonstrate this through all facets of life.

27 SUNDAY ☿ *Moon Age Day 23 Moon Sign Leo*

am...

pm...

The challenge today is to keep one step ahead of the competition. This is as true at work as it is in more social or sporting situations. Don't be surprised if not everyone proves to be adept at expressing either their opinions or their wishes today. A good deal of second-guessing may be necessary in order to address the situation.

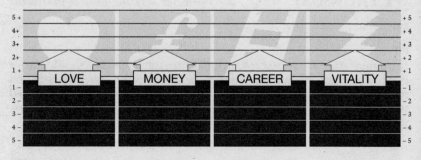

28 MONDAY ☿ *Moon Age Day 24 Moon Sign Leo*

am ....

pm..

There are new highlights on offer in love and romance. This might come as something of a shock to some Librans, particularly those who have placed such considerations firmly on the back burner during the last couple of weeks. The best way to avoid lethargy today is to pitch in and boost your own sense of achievement.

29 TUESDAY ☿ *Moon Age Day 25 Moon Sign Leo*

am ....

pm..

You could find a degree of restlessness pervading your life as October draws towards its close. Your best response is to find something different to do and maybe some alternative people to share events and activities with you. This part of the week can be interesting, though once again it depends on how much effort you put in.

30 WEDNESDAY ☿ *Moon Age Day 26 Moon Sign Virgo*

am ....

pm..

The planetary focus today is on your presently strong personality and the way others view it. Even those you mix with frequently may not be used to seeing the very determined Libra, so it's worth giving them a sign to let them know you haven't really changed at all. Nevertheless, remain specific in your intentions.

31 THURSDAY ☿ *Moon Age Day 27 Moon Sign Virgo*

am ....

pm..

Acquiring what you need from life generally represents one of your greatest strengths at present. This can be a very practical period and one during which the focus is on your energy and your irrepressible desire to succeed. If you can't take everyone down the road you want to follow, why not go it alone?

1 FRIDAY ☿ *Moon Age Day 28 Moon Sign Libra*

am..
pm..

Stand by to take advantage of a potentially lucky period. With the lunar high comes a sudden surge in the power of Mercury in your life. This assists you to talk with confidence, walk with certainty and attract a number of admirers. By all means give yourself a pat on the back for something you've done well – then move on!

2 SATURDAY ☿ *Moon Age Day 0 Moon Sign Libra*

am..
pm..

The lunar high encourages you to redress a few balances and promotes a more centred attitude. Contacts with others should be less strained, and you can utilise the strong diplomatic skills that are the province of your zodiac sign. When it comes to money, you can afford to chance your arm at the moment.

3 SUNDAY ☿ *Moon Age Day 1 Moon Sign Scorpio*

am..
pm..

Current planetary trends assist you to show your best qualities and help you to create a supportive, stable atmosphere, which is ideal for a Sunday. You have scope to find comfort at home, and might decide to put to one side that need for movement that has been so much a part of your nature across the last few weeks.

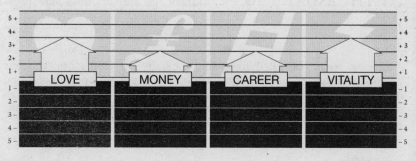

November

2013

YOUR MONTH AT A GLANCE

(+) = Opportunities are around   ● = Be on the defensive   ● = Life is pretty ordinary

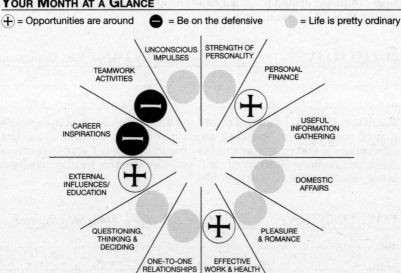

UNCONSCIOUS IMPULSES

STRENGTH OF PERSONALITY

TEAMWORK ACTIVITIES

PERSONAL FINANCE

CAREER INSPIRATIONS

USEFUL INFORMATION GATHERING

EXTERNAL INFLUENCES/ EDUCATION

DOMESTIC AFFAIRS

QUESTIONING, THINKING & DECIDING

PLEASURE & ROMANCE

ONE-TO-ONE RELATIONSHIPS

EFFECTIVE WORK & HEALTH

NOVEMBER HIGHS AND LOWS

Here I show you how the rhythms of the Moon will affect you this month. Like the tide, your energies and abilities will rise and fall with its pattern. When it is above the centre line, go for it, when it is below, you should be resting. **HIGH** 1ST–2ND   **HIGH** 28TH–30TH

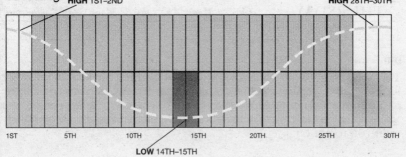

1ST   5TH   10TH   15TH   20TH   25TH   30TH

LOW 14TH–15TH

4 MONDAY ☿ *Moon Age Day 2 Moon Sign Scorpio*

am ....

pm..

There is no reason to hang back when it comes to good ideas. Simply put your mind to the task of inventing new possibilities. You are still in the mood to get ahead, and it's simply a question of finding people around who can be persuaded to lend a hand. Romance is available for young or young-at-heart Librans.

5 TUESDAY ☿ *Moon Age Day 3 Moon Sign Sagittarius*

am ....

pm..

There is nothing to be gained by making life difficult for others, especially that of your partner. Spending time on your own can work wonders, particularly if you're not in the best frame of mind. Creative potential continues to be well accented, and you can use this to cheer up your home or even to tackle a new hobby.

6 WEDNESDAY ☿ *Moon Age Day 4 Moon Sign Sagittarius*

am ....

pm..

This would be an ideal time to seek new answers to old problems, since your ability to think things through is to the fore. You are also in a position to increase your level of popularity. Prepare to identify those around you who share your enthusiasm for life, and convince them to join in and have fun with you.

7 THURSDAY ☿ *Moon Age Day 5 Moon Sign Capricorn*

am ....

pm..

The Sun, presently in your solar second house, is a favourable influence for building on fresh starts that are already under way, or plans you choose to put into action now. At work you need to consider the impression you are making on superiors. Remember, there other people who genuinely want you to get on.

8 FRIDAY   ☿   *Moon Age Day 6 Moon Sign Capricorn*

am ....

pm..

Your best approach to professional obligations today is to proceed in a quiet and organised way. Social matters are a different matter! Once the necessary routines are out of the way, you have a chance to let your hair down and have a good time. In a financial sense it's a question of discovering ways to gain more control.

9 SATURDAY   ☿   *Moon Age Day 7 Moon Sign Aquarius*

am ....

pm..

Do you feel there hasn't been time of late to do everything you had wished? Even if today is busy too, you ought to be able to spare some moments to do someone a good turn. Offering help and advice is part of the Libra nature, and today is no exception. The company of younger people might hold a particular appeal.

10 SUNDAY   ☿   *Moon Age Day 8 Moon Sign Aquarius*

am ....

pm..

A potentially quieter day allows you to mull over events from the past. This tinge of nostalgia is fine, as long as you don't become too tied up with retrospective thinking. Social highlights are available later, and there is much to be said for taking the opportunity to focus on your commitment to family members.

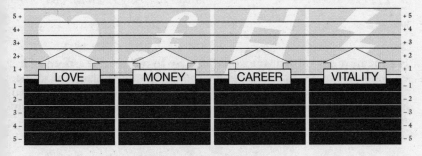

11 MONDAY ☿ *Moon Age Day 9 Moon Sign Aquarius*

am ....

pm ....

Any minor hitches early in the day could simply prove to you that the strictly practical is not your most favoured area this week. Life now is about going along with others and mixing different potentials to ensure that everyone has a good time. This would be an ideal day for shopping, and for showing that you have an eye for a bargain!

12 TUESDAY *Moon Age Day 10 Moon Sign Pisces*

am ....

pm ....

The go-getting side of your nature should be more apparent today. Despite this, your sensitivity is also enhanced, especially in terms of the needs of both older and younger people. Showing that you are a good listener is part of what the day is about. As well as assisting others, you can gain much along the way.

13 WEDNESDAY *Moon Age Day 11 Moon Sign Pisces*

am ....

pm ....

If you insist on keeping the pace of everyday life as brisk as ever, finding time to simply be yourself could be quite difficult. Don't get hung up about Christmas just yet, even if the world is telling you that it is just around the corner. The more variety you can bring into your life today, the better you should feel.

14 THURSDAY *Moon Age Day 12 Moon Sign Aries*

am ....

pm ....

For the next day or two you would be wise to put specific aspects of life on hold. Although there's nothing wrong with thinking big, the chance of actually moving forward is not helped by the presence of the lunar low. This is one occasion on which putting things off for a few days can work wonders.

15 FRIDAY
Moon Age Day 13 Moon Sign Aries

am ....

pm..

A new period of domestic rewards is on offer. Venus gives you every assistance to get on especially well with family members and to gain from their company. This would be an ideal opportunity to address any recent tensions at home and to find ways to put them right once and for all.

16 SATURDAY
Moon Age Day 14 Moon Sign Taurus

am ....

pm..

Social discussions and meetings can now bring enlightenment, and it's worth seeking the company of interesting types. New friendships become possible at this time, and there may also be a renewed fresh approach to existing ties. Almost anyone could have the ability to move you because you are presently so sensitive.

17 SUNDAY
Moon Age Day 15 Moon Sign Taurus

am ....

pm..

The further you are able to go today, the better you should feel. This is true in terms of actual journeys you might choose to take, but also with regard to specific issues that you decide to push beyond previous limits. You needn't allow anyone or anything to hold you back during this most important interlude.

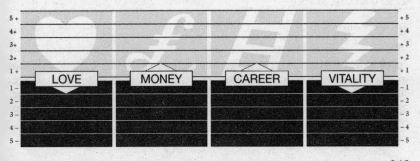

18 MONDAY   *Moon Age Day 16 Moon Sign Taurus*

am ....

pm...

Professional matters can be a real labour of love today, which can be some consolation if they are not offering too much in the way of financial remuneration. Be patient, as you will have a chance to improve monetary matters in due course – but not just yet. All the same, be sure to check your lottery ticket carefully!

19 TUESDAY   *Moon Age Day 17 Moon Sign Gemini*

am ....

pm...

There is a warning around today not to listen to the tall tales of others, and at the same time be careful you are not spreading any gossip yourself. If you need to know something, it would be far better to check out the details directly. You can be quite creative now, and should be willing to use this in all your daily tasks.

20 WEDNESDAY   *Moon Age Day 18 Moon Sign Gemini*

am ....

pm...

As far as personal and emotional security are concerned, today is about ensuring you are well looked after. In terms of your nature, you have what it takes to be charming and well co-ordinated at the moment – with just the right attitude that is necessary to get on well in life. Don't forget to show your wisdom too.

21 THURSDAY   *Moon Age Day 19 Moon Sign Cancer*

am ....

pm...

In practical matters, you need to keep your eye on the ball. This is not a time to diversify too much, and concentration is all-important. If you feel that family members are not taking their own responsibilities quite as seriously as they should, this might be the right time to let them know – gently!

22 FRIDAY
Moon Age Day 20 Moon Sign Cancer

am ....

pm..

You can use your home situation to help you redress the balance at work, particularly if you are extremely active. Use some of your spare hours to quite simply have a rest and don't take on any more tasks than are strictly necessary at this time. Avoid getting on the wrong side of anyone who is in a position of influence.

23 SATURDAY
Moon Age Day 21 Moon Sign Leo

am ....

pm..

A combination of leisure and romance ought to appeal today, in those moments when you are not busy working. If you want to avoid becoming bored, it would be sensible to deliberately make alterations to your routines. There is no point in worrying too much at the moment, unless it's about a lack of excitement.

24 SUNDAY
Moon Age Day 22 Moon Sign Leo

am ....

pm..

With the Sun having moved from the second to the third house of your chart, this is the best time of all to allow yourself to be utterly ambitious in your attitude. A favourable weekend to focus clearly on a range of issues, including the direction your life is taking. For the moment it pays to think, but not act.

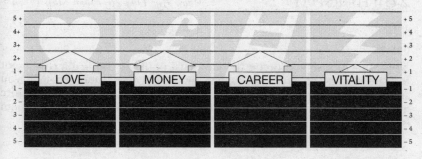

25 MONDAY

Moon Age Day 23 Moon Sign Leo

am ....

pm ....

Now you should be able to get your ideas across to others and to make a positive impression on the world at large. It could feel as though you have suddenly heard the starter's gun, as you race ahead, particularly in practical matters. Romantically speaking, letting someone know how you feel is the name of the game.

26 TUESDAY

Moon Age Day 24 Moon Sign Virgo

am ....

pm ....

It is possible that you are less socially inclined today, probably because the Moon is in your solar twelfth house. This encourages an interlude that is far quieter than of late – and more contemplative too. Be sure to let close friends, as well as your partner, know that you are not sulking about anything.

27 WEDNESDAY

Moon Age Day 25 Moon Sign Virgo

am ....

pm ....

This is a better time than most if you have decided to retreat from events a little and think things through more deeply. Of course the world makes certain demands of you that you cannot avoid, but meditation should still be possible. Ask others to take some of the strain and recharge flagging batteries.

28 THURSDAY

Moon Age Day 26 Moon Sign Libra

am ....

pm ....

Now your foot should be on the gas pedal of life as you begin to move forward in a very progressive way. The lunar high offers better general luck and ways to utilise all those good ideas that are floating around in your mind. Taking the odd chance can be fun, though financial speculation isn't to be recommended.

29 FRIDAY

Moon Age Day 27 Moon Sign Libra

am ....

pm ....

You have a chance to make yourself the centre of attention today, which is why it would be sensible to line up in your mind all those things you would wish others to do for you. It isn't being selfish to make use of your popularity, and in any case most of the people you approach for help should be more than happy to oblige.

30 SATURDAY

Moon Age Day 28 Moon Sign Libra

am ....

pm ....

Make sure colleagues and friends notice how talkative, inquisitive and extremely friendly you are at the moment. The level of good luck available is still high, assisting you to go a step further than would normally be the case. Love and romance wait around the corner for Librans who are actively seeking either.

1 SUNDAY

Moon Age Day 29 Moon Sign Scorpio

am ....

pm ....

You can definitely benefit from getting out and about. Being held in the same place all the time will probably hold little appeal at present, and you can afford to be quite definite in your attitude regarding personal freedom. If you make sure the people you meet today understand your point of view, they are more likely to offer support.

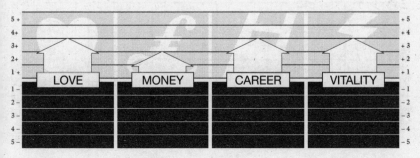

December 2013

YOUR MONTH AT A GLANCE

(+) = Opportunities are around   ● = Be on the defensive   ● = Life is pretty ordinary

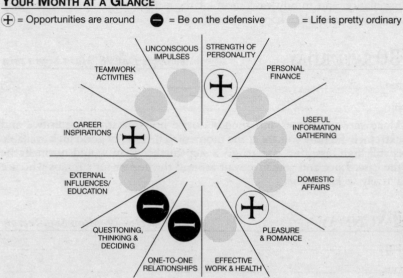

STRENGTH OF PERSONALITY

UNCONSCIOUS IMPULSES

PERSONAL FINANCE

TEAMWORK ACTIVITIES

USEFUL INFORMATION GATHERING

CAREER INSPIRATIONS

EXTERNAL INFLUENCES/ EDUCATION

DOMESTIC AFFAIRS

QUESTIONING, THINKING & DECIDING

PLEASURE & ROMANCE

ONE-TO-ONE RELATIONSHIPS

EFFECTIVE WORK & HEALTH

DECEMBER HIGHS AND LOWS

Here I show you how the rhythms of the Moon will affect you this month. Like the tide, your energies and abilities will rise and fall with its pattern. When it is above the centre line, go for it, when it is below, you should be resting.

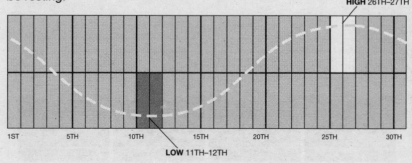

HIGH 26TH–27TH

1ST   5TH   10TH   15TH   20TH   25TH   30TH

LOW 11TH–12TH

2 MONDAY
Moon Age Day 0 Moon Sign Scorpio

am..

pm..

There are signs that Libra could be taking an 'easy come, easy go' attitude towards money at present. This is probably just as well because, with Christmas close at hand, there's a risk of spending more than you intended. Be prepared to take some time out to really understand what makes your partner tick.

3 TUESDAY
Moon Age Day 1 Moon Sign Sagittarius

am..

pm..

Teamwork matters count for a great deal at present, which is why you should be willing to co-operate, even with people you haven't seen eye to eye with in the past. You can't expect to get everything you want from life at present, especially in a financial sense, though you might get close in at least some cases.

4 WEDNESDAY
Moon Age Day 2 Moon Sign Sagittarius

am..

pm..

When it comes to wit and intelligence, it appears that few can better you at present, and this can definitely help to boost your popularity. Such a trend has to be good with Christmas just around the corner, and it might also assist some Libran subjects in their efforts to advance at work.

5 THURSDAY
Moon Age Day 3 Moon Sign Capricorn

am..

pm..

A potentially hectic period in your personal life begins around this time. Of course, Christmas is fast approaching, and you might be starting to get in the mood, even though it's only the start of the month. Socially speaking, fighting shy of people you don't know very well would be understandable just now.

6 FRIDAY

Moon Age Day 4 Moon Sign Capricorn

am ....

pm ....

Keep your eyes and ears open for significant new input today and don't turn down the chance to do something different. The spotlight is on your curiosity, your instinctive need to know what makes things tick, so getting to the very heart of any matter is likely to be a priority. A day to show others how fascinating you can be.

7 SATURDAY

Moon Age Day 5 Moon Sign Aquarius

am ....

pm ....

Personal and intimate matters give you the chance to show your best side at this time. Concentrating on the family, rather than distant friends or even work, would certainly be no bad thing. If you find yourself facing a mountain of work, the best approach is to break it down into easily manageable units.

8 SUNDAY

Moon Age Day 6 Moon Sign Aquarius

am ....

pm ....

Even on a Sunday, professional demands could be quite irritating, especially if you have to deal with people who appear to be hopeless. Your usual Libran patience should be present, though perhaps not in great measure. What will work is your sense of humour. It's time to find laughter in every situation.

	LOVE	MONEY	CAREER	VITALITY

9 MONDAY

Moon Age Day 7 Moon Sign Pisces

am ....

pm..

What you may find out in group situations today could prove to be extremely useful in the end. Listen to what is being said and don't commit yourself to joining in unless you are very sure of your ground. If you feel particularly fatigued at this time, there is nothing at all wrong with taking a short break.

10 TUESDAY

Moon Age Day 8 Moon Sign Pisces

am ....

pm..

You can now benefit from the diversity of interests that are so typical of the Air-sign Libran nature. With more energy at your disposal and the chance to put it to good use, this is an ideal time to tackle all manner of new jobs. Your willingness to offer help and advice to others is noteworthy at the moment.

11 WEDNESDAY

Moon Age Day 9 Moon Sign Aries

am ....

pm..

Confidence could sag somewhat as the lunar low arrives, but you don't have to give in to this tendency. Decide from the start that you are going to enjoy this quieter period and to use it to the best of your ability. Quiet pursuits are the order of the day, and can bring a degree of relaxation and even joy.

12 THURSDAY

Moon Age Day 10 Moon Sign Aries

am ....

pm..

You need to be prepared to contend with certain limitations at the present time. This may not go down well, particularly if you are feeling a great deal of urgency within your nature at this time. Try to go with the flow in social matters, and listen specifically to what others are saying in family situations.

13 FRIDAY
Moon Age Day 11 Moon Sign Taurus

am ....

pm ....

This has potential to be a more than agreeable period. Venus is strong in your solar chart, assisting you to promote good relations in and around your home and domestic life. This is a very positive influence to have approaching Christmas time, and can be especially useful if you wish to create a traditional festive celebration.

14 SATURDAY
Moon Age Day 12 Moon Sign Taurus

am ....

pm ....

There is a very strong concern today with getting things done. Maybe you are too caught up with the details and fail to notice the importance of the sheer effort you are putting in? You need time to contemplate your actions and to come to terms with the slightly altered perceptions of loved ones.

15 SUNDAY
Moon Age Day 13 Moon Sign Taurus

am ....

pm ....

Emotional rewards are now there for the taking. In discussions related to work you will need to have the courage of your convictions, though this is not necessarily the case at home. It's important to finish off any outstanding tasks and, if possible, make the most of social possibilities that are on offer this evening.

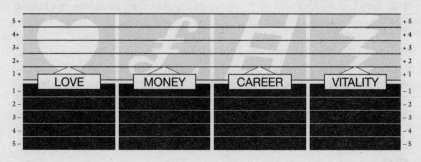

16 MONDAY
Moon Age Day 14 Moon Sign Gemini

am ....

pm ....

Beware of overestimating your capacity for work. Although you have plenty of energy available in general this month, there are signs that today could be an exception. Why not pace yourself and allow others to take some of the strain? Remember that you need time to recover – ready for tomorrow's exertions!

17 TUESDAY
Moon Age Day 15 Moon Sign Gemini

am ....

pm ....

If you are faced with any slightly risky situations, you can afford to back your intuition at the moment. It isn't like Libra to take great chances, but you may decide that calculated ones are acceptable. There is also a focus today on money matters, and on how you deal with the necessities of Christmas.

18 WEDNESDAY
Moon Age Day 16 Moon Sign Cancer

am ....

pm ....

Trends encourage fruitful encounters with a number of different individuals today, some of whom may be able to offer the sort of information that is both timely and useful. Where love and romance are concerned, it shouldn't be difficult to find the right words to sweep someone off their feet under present planetary influences.

19 THURSDAY
Moon Age Day 17 Moon Sign Cancer

am ....

pm ....

A sense of urgency is all very well, but it could be misplaced today. It's important to recognise the progress you are making in various aspects of life, even if some of them are not coming good quite as quickly as you wish. Stay aware of the needs of family members, especially those of your partner.

20 FRIDAY

Moon Age Day 18 Moon Sign Cancer

am ....

pm...

You have a chance to gain great fulfilment today through your family. Getting on positively in terms of your career is a different matter, though you should be able to address any problems in this area. Socially speaking, it's time for Libra to get the festive season well under way!

21 SATURDAY

Moon Age Day 19 Moon Sign Leo

am ....

pm...

Your fun-loving nature is stimulated by present planetary trends, giving you the opportunity to show the joker inside you at almost every turn. There's no reason to hold back in any situation, simply because you doubt the reaction of colleagues. If you have things to say, you can persuade the world to lend an ear.

22 SUNDAY

Moon Age Day 20 Moon Sign Leo

am ....

pm...

You can take advantage of an influx of bright new ideas, and need to ensure you have a positive audience. Your usual ways of relaxing might not fit the bill at present, and it is entirely possible that you will be looking for new ways to pep up your social hours, particularly this evening.

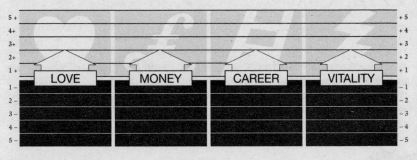

23 MONDAY
Moon Age Day 21 Moon Sign Virgo

am ....

pm..

Emotive issues in relationships take centre stage for some Libran subjects today. Don't be too ready to allow these a great deal of room in your mind. It is possible that you are not being anywhere near as rational as you could be. Once again, you need to take a longer-term view of situations.

24 TUESDAY
Moon Age Day 22 Moon Sign Virgo

am ....

pm..

This certainly has potential to be a very positive time when it comes to pleasing family members and friends alike. All the same, you can consider this to be your special day during the Christmas break, and it's worth finding ways to do the things that really appeal to you. This might include spending at least some time alone.

25 WEDNESDAY
Moon Age Day 23 Moon Sign Virgo

am ....

pm..

Be willing to open your eyes to something wonderful today, despite the necessary tasks of a Christmas Day. If you're spending time with family members, turning your mind to future holidays would be no bad thing. Whatever you are thinking today, there is a long-term aspect about it that brightens the day no end.

26 THURSDAY
Moon Age Day 24 Moon Sign Libra

am ....

pm..

If ever there was a time when it was possible for you to talk anyone into anything, that day has come. The lunar high, together with Mercury's position in your solar chart, enhances your silver tongue and your tremendous influence. Now is the time to feather your own nest materially, and to help others on the way.

27 FRIDAY
Moon Age Day 25 Moon Sign Libra

am ....

pm ....

Another family high spot when you can allow your sense of absolute joy to shine out like the sun. You can capitalise on your popularity at this time, which is always stimulating to the Libran personality. In the full swing of the party season, this is no time to be running out of steam or seeking places to be quiet.

28 SATURDAY
Moon Age Day 26 Moon Sign Scorpio

am ....

pm ....

Group-based activities may hold some potential rewards. There are some frustrations to be dealt with now, particularly if you are unable to get the world going in the way you would wish until after the beginning of the New Year. The Christmas break can seem too long for all the Air signs, of which you are one.

29 SUNDAY
Moon Age Day 27 Moon Sign Scorpio

am ....

pm ....

Relationships could well have their ups and downs at the moment, and it's worth asking yourself whether you have been spending too much time in the company of one specific individual. The spotlight is also on your level of consumption. Abstinence is not necessary, though a little circumspection might help.

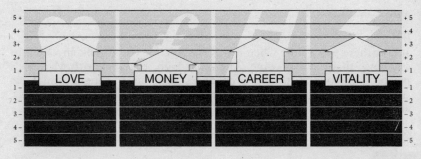

30 MONDAY

Moon Age Day 28 Moon Sign Sagittarius

am ....

pm ....

It's important to mix with as many different sorts of people today as proves to be possible. You have a chance to come up with a number of quite innovative ideas. The next step is to find individuals who will listen to what you have to say and who can even be persuaded to help you to push forward progressively.

31 TUESDAY

Moon Age Day 29 Moon Sign Sagittarius

am ....

pm ....

The last day of the year offers an opportunity to create fun and diversity. The emphasis is now firmly on humour, conversation and good company, and it's up to you to seek out all of these. Beware of taking anything too seriously at present, and be willing to enjoy whatever party is taking place.

RISING SIGNS FOR LIBRA

SEPTEMBER | OCTOBER

LEO
VIRGO
LIBRA
SCORPIO
SAGITTARIUS
CAPRICORN
AQUARIUS
PISCES
ARIES
TAURUS
GEMINI
CANCER
LEO

MIDNIGHT
AM
MIDDAY
PM

158

THE ZODIAC, PLANETS AND CORRESPONDENCES

The Earth revolves around the Sun once every calendar year, so when viewed from Earth the Sun appears in a different part of the sky as the year progresses. In astrology, these parts of the sky are divided into the signs of the zodiac and this means that the signs are organised in a circle. The circle begins with Aries and ends with Pisces.

Taking the zodiac sign as a starting point, astrologers then work with all the positions of planets, stars and many other factors to calculate horoscopes and birth charts and tell us what the stars have in store for us.

The table below shows the planets and Elements for each of the signs of the zodiac. Each sign belongs to one of the four Elements: Fire, Air, Earth or Water. Fire signs are creative and enthusiastic; Air signs are mentally active and thoughtful; Earth signs are constructive and practical; Water signs are emotional and have strong feelings.

It also shows the metals and gemstones associated with, or corresponding with, each sign. The correspondence is made when a metal or stone possesses properties that are held in common with a particular sign of the zodiac.

Finally, the table shows the opposite of each star sign – this is the opposite sign in the astrological circle.

Placed	Sign	Symbol	Element	Planet	Metal	Stone	Opposite
1	Aries	Ram	Fire	Mars	Iron	Bloodstone	Libra
2	Taurus	Bull	Earth	Venus	Copper	Sapphire	Scorpio
3	Gemini	Twins	Air	Mercury	Mercury	Tiger's Eye	Sagittarius
4	Cancer	Crab	Water	Moon	Silver	Pearl	Capricorn
5	Leo	Lion	Fire	Sun	Gold	Ruby	Aquarius
6	Virgo	Maiden	Earth	Mercury	Mercury	Sardonyx	Pisces
7	Libra	Scales	Air	Venus	Copper	Sapphire	Aries
8	Scorpio	Scorpion	Water	Pluto	Plutonium	Jasper	Taurus
9	Sagittarius	Archer	Fire	Jupiter	Tin	Topaz	Gemini
10	Capricorn	Goat	Earth	Saturn	Lead	Black Onyx	Cancer
11	Aquarius	Waterbearer	Air	Uranus	Uranium	Amethyst	Leo
12	Pisces	Fishes	Water	Neptune	Tin	Moonstone	Virgo

TALISMAN OF THE SEVEN ANGELS

Created by the Circle of Raphael

Invite Seven Angels into Your Life Today with the Aid of this Lucky Angelic Pendant Talisman of the Seven Angels. ONLY £21.50 plus p&p.

Individually crafted in solid sterling silver. Order today and receive a FREE chain.

Angels are highly positive Cosmic beings and they will not usually step into a person's life without first being invited to do so. This Angelic lucky pendant, inscribed in the divine Angelic language of the Cosmos and imbued with the sacred holy words of creation, was revealed to the Mystic of the *Circle of Raphael* by the Angels themselves. The sacred holy words and Angel names embedded in the pendant are what make it so special. Ownership of this lucky Angelic prayer pendant invites each one of the Seven Angels to befriend its owner and bless and protect them. Over the years we have received numerous testimonials in the form of letters and emails from extremely pleased and astounded owners of this lucky Angelic pendant. To view our genuine testimonials please visit our website.

To fulfil their own spiritual destiny, Angels need to give of themselves and assist anyone who requests their help. However, they first need you to personally invite them into your life so they can fulfil their divine purpose. The most direct and successful way of inviting Angels into your life is to simply wear or carry this holy Angelic pendant calling on the Seven Angels using their personal holy name asking each of them to befriend, watch over and protect the wearer every day of their life. The following is a list of the Angelic gifts associated with each of the Seven Angels named on the pendant plus the true holy name of each Angel written in Angelic script and translated into English:

(ט) ZAPHAEL – Inner peace and happiness.

(ר) GABRIEL – Divine protection and safety in travel.

(ל) HANIEL – Luck in love and relationships.

(ה) RAPHAEL – Financial security and good health.

(ק) CHAMAEL – Protection from acts of violence.

(מ) ZADKIEL – Good fortune in games of chance.

(ז) MICHAEL – Angelic help in career and work.

Wear or carry this lucky Angelic prayer in the form of a pendant and personally invite the Seven Angels to befriend you and enter your life. This one lucky Angelic pendant also invites all Seven Angels to act as your personal Angelic ally in times of need.

We charge only one £4.50 postage & packing fee no matter how many pendants you order at the same time for delivery to the same address. So why not order an extra one for a friend or loved one and save on the postage? **To order by post:** Send your name and address plus your cheque, postal order or debit/credit card details **made payable to: C.O. Raphael.**

Send to: C.O. RAPHAEL (OMH) P.O. BOX 73, ST AUSTELL, PL26 8SH, UK

UK Postage & Packing: Please add £4.50 to your order. **Airmail P&P Outside UK:** Add £8.00 to your order. Do **NOT** send cash under any circumstances.

FAST ORDER ONLINE AT:

www.circleraphael.co.uk

Order With Confidence – This miraculous Seven Angel pendant is covered by our unique 60-day guarantee of full satisfaction or your money back – less the postage & packing fee paid.